ridiculous / hilarious / terrible / cool

ridiculous / hilarious / terrible / cool

a year in an american high school

elisha cooper

 dial  books

Dial Books
A member of Penguin Group (USA) Inc.
Published by The Penguin Group
Penguin Group (USA) Inc., 375 Hudson Street, New York, NY 10014, U.S.A.
Penguin Group (Canada), 90 Eglinton Avenue East, Suite 700,
Toronto, Ontario, Canada M4P 2Y3 (a division of Pearson Penguin Canada Inc.)
Penguin Books Ltd, 80 Strand, London WC2R 0RL, England
Penguin Ireland, 25 St. Stephen's Green, Dublin 2, Ireland
(a division of Penguin Books Ltd)
Penguin Group (Australia), 250 Camberwell Road, Camberwell,
Victoria 3124, Australia (a division of Pearson Australia Group Pty Ltd)
Penguin Books India Pvt Ltd, 11 Community Centre,
Panchsheel Park, New Delhi - 110 017, India
Penguin Group (NZ), 67 Apollo Drive, Rosedale,
North Shore 0632, New Zealand (a division of Pearson New Zealand Ltd)
Penguin Books (South Africa) (Pty) Ltd, 24 Sturdee Avenue,
Rosebank, Johannesburg 2196, South Africa
Penguin Books Ltd, Registered Offices: 80 Strand, London WC2R 0RL, England

The publisher does not have any control over and does not assume any
responsibility for author or third-party websites or their content.
Designed by Lily Malcom
Text set in Garamond 3
Printed in the U.S.A.
10 9 8 7 6 5 4 3 2 1

Library of Congress Cataloging-in-Publication Data

Cooper, Elisha.
Ridiculous/hilarious/terrible/cool : a year in an American high school / Elisha Cooper.
    p. cm.
ISBN: 978-0-8037-3169-1
1. High school students—Illinois—Chicago—Juvenile literature.
2. High schools—Illinois—Chicago—Juvenile literature.
I. Title: Ridiculous, hilarious, terrible, cool. II. Title.

LA269.C4C56 2008
373.180977311—dc22
                            2007024533

Some individuals in the book have requested that their names be changed. Some names have been changed
to protect identities. In a few instances, the timeline of events has been rearranged for clarity.

for 1989

This is the dawning of the rest of our lives

— Green Day

SEPTEMBER

On the first day of school, Daniel Patton wakes at 5:15. Then he hits the snooze button. At 6:15 he wakes for good, showers, and puts on a blue pinstripe shirt, new jeans, and clean white sneakers.

At 6:30 he's out the door and striding past the rough brick houses of the South Side. The streets are deserted, the corner store still locked. Daniel boards his bus, taking a seat in the back so he can stretch his long legs. As the bus accelerates up the lake, the skyline of downtown Chicago shimmers on the horizon.

When the bus enters the Loop, Daniel transfers to the subway.

He gets off three stops later and buys a bagel to go. Heading west in his loping gait, Daniel—a lanky African American teenager with cropped hair, black-rimmed glasses, and a backpack over his shoulder—looks exactly like a high school class president, which, in fact, he is.

Daniel is excited for his senior year. He's excited to be a leader of his high school, excited for his classes, excited to be applying to college. He's especially excited about applying to Harvard.

Then Daniel takes a left turn, and there is his school: Walter Payton College Preparatory High School. As the brick walls of the school come into focus, Daniel quickens his pace. A year of possibility stretches in front of him.

Payton sits in an athletic field like a block of butter on a green plate. Its walls are a cream brick, broken by tall windows that reach up to a curving metallic roof. The surrounding field has soccer goals, a baseball diamond, bushes and trees growing against the sides of the building. West of the school, past the rusted steel ribbon of the elevated train tracks, the Cabrini Green Housing Projects loom, countless concrete buildings in various states of demolition. East of the school, past steel and brick condos under construction, rise the skyscrapers of downtown Chicago. Payton is wedged between these two worlds.

Payton is a new high school, a magnet that draws students from all over the city. The students divide roughly along racial lines: a third black, a third white, a third Latino, with a smaller percentage who are Asian. Payton is a selective public high school, created as an academic urban alternative to the suburban high schools. They have a motto: "We nurture leaders." They have a mascot: the Grizzly. They have an address—1034

North Wells Street—which intentionally contains the number (34) of the legendary Chicago Bears running back for whom Payton is named.

Today, on the first day of school, students gather outside the front door, looking as fresh and polished as their building. Or at least, freshly resolved. This year, this is what I am going to *be*. Then the doors open and the students surge past the security desk, and into the high school.

Emily Harris walks through the halls as if she were knocking people out of the way. Leading with the right shoulder, then the left. The expression on her face could knock people over too.

She doesn't look to either side of her. Doesn't look at the red lockers, the beige brick walls, the trophy cases packed with Walter Payton memorabilia: photographs of Walter playing football, balls that Walter signed, the box of Wheaties with Walter on the front. She doesn't even look at the bust of Walter outside the administration offices. Her eyes stay focused straight ahead.

Emily's eyes are intense and brown, her skin the color of cocoa. Her curly black hair is pulled tight in a ponytail that hangs over strong shoulders, which today are sport-

4

ing a yellow T-shirt that reads *brasil*. Emily is captain of the Payton girls' soccer team.

Emily has goals for her team. As a junior, when she was also captain, Emily led the Grizzlies to the regional finals in States. This year the Grizzlies will move to a larger division and play the best high schools in Illinois. Emily's goal is to lead her team to the finals. She welcomes the challenge, welcomes the responsibility. She will coordinate conditioning, organize indoor games in the winter, everything leading to a successful spring season.

Emily has her own goals too. She's been All-City, All-Conference, All-Section, almost every year since she was a freshman. She's won team awards for leadership, for being a scholar athlete. She's been the team MVP. She's scored countless goals and had even more assists. She plans to match these successes and top them this year. And then, of course, there's college.

"Hey!" shouts a friend, and Emily's serious face breaks into a big toothy grin, wide and infectious, as if she just ripped a ball into the back of the net and were acknowledging the cheering crowd.

5

After talking with her friend, back goes the serious face. Emily stops at her locker before swinging herself down the hall again, right shoulder, left shoulder, right. Then she sees another friend and cocks her foot and kicks her in the rear end.

At 9:04, the bell rings for class, and a river of students streams through school as if the gates on a dam were opened. The students splash down stairs, gurgle up stairs, rush from class to class, and flood the atrium.

Payton centers around its atrium, an airy three-story-high space in the middle of the school. Everything opens on the atrium: the library, the gym, the recital hall, the cafeteria, the classrooms, the administration offices, the hallways. Wide windows grace each end of the atrium. In its middle are two stairways: one up, one down.

Security guards hover at the stairs. In their orange and blue Payton sweatshirts, they look like the students, though twenty years older and fifty pounds heavier. As they swipe at baseball hats and growl at anyone trying to go up the down staircase, they look like bears in a waterfall swatting at salmon.

Then at 9:08 the bell rings again. And, as if the gates on the dam were closed, the last drops of students race up and down the stairs, books clutched to their chests, late for class. The guards shout: "Let's go. Let's *go*. Where we supposed to *be*?!"

Maya Boudreau sits in her AP English class on the third floor, fidgeting. She has a fidgeting routine. It starts with her right foot, rolled clockwise. Then her left foot, rolled counter-clockwise. Then she sucks her cheeks in, pouts her full lips, smoothes her hands, and starts rolling her foot again. Some-times, to vary the routine, Maya chews her hair.

Maya has long brown hair and pretty Midwestern features. She looks like the proverbial girl next door, if next door were the twenty-sixth floor of the downtown apartment building along Lake Shore Drive where Maya lives with her family. But Maya does have a small-town affect. The big wide eyes, the careful note-taking. She could play the role of The Good Student.

Maya has performed in countless productions at Payton and has the reputation as *the* actor in school. She's acted in a youth program at Steppenwolf Theatre, taught acting over the sum-mer at the Lookingglass Theatre. When she daydreams in class, which is often, she pictures herself in New York, acting on the stage and living a romantic life. Sometimes, of course, she just daydreams about boys.

7

Even with Maya's fidgeting, the other kids in class are fidgeting more. It's as if the entire class has Tourette's. The shaggy-haired boy to Maya's right tugs on his soul patch so hard it looks painful. The shaggy-haired boy to Maya's left drums on the part of his hairy belly that's peeking out from his shirt. Across from Maya, a skinny boy with big ears flips a pencil. The girl next to him bites her fingernails until they bleed. The boy next to her picks his nose, and when no one is looking, wipes what he got out on his socks.

The only one in the classroom not fidgeting is their English teacher, Ms. Murphy. Though, her hair sort of fidgets. Red and frizzy, it bounces above her with a mind of its own, spiraling toward the ceiling and toward the theater-poster-covered walls, as the person beneath it circles the room and makes her introductions for the year.

Maya watches and rolls her foot, daydreaming about New York.

On the front of each Payton ID is the student's photo, her class and lunch period, everything laminated and fastened to an orange and blue lanyard. Some students wear their lanyard backward, some hang their lanyard in their pants pocket, some substitute their own lanyards. Not Diana Martinez. She wears hers correctly, her ID around her neck. Diana's ID has her photo: round face, dark eyes, thick hair. Her class: senior. Her lunch period: fifth. Her ID does not show her roundish body or plain clothes. As she sits quietly in her classes, she does not invite attention.

When teachers ask questions, Diana answers in her head. Sometimes she feels intimidated by the smart students in class, the ones who answer everything. As they talk, she watches. She often finds that the smart kids say, word for word, what she was thinking, but she still rarely raises her hand to speak.

When Diana does speak outside of class, she does so carefully in the not-quite-accurate speech of someone for whom the language does not come easily, something she seems aware of and makes allowances for. Instead of "Yeah," she says "Yes," with each of the three letters carefully enunciated: *"Ye-eh-es."* She always talks with a small smile on her face.

Diana speaks Spanish at home with her parents, English with her siblings. Her father drives the night-shift forklift for a trucking company. Her mother runs the house and takes care of Diana's younger brother. Diana's twin sisters are one year older than she is, and just graduated from a high school in their West Side neighborhood that is entirely Mexican. They tease Diana for going to a "white" school. They think Diana is "book smart, street stupid," and think they themselves are "book stupid, street smart." Neither sister works. Diana has an older brother and he doesn't work either.

Diana thinks her sisters are being unfair. Nothing is that simple. Diana doesn't feel so stupid about life, or so smart about books. It's not as if schoolwork comes without difficulty.

She wants to go to college. She also wants to hang out with her friends. She wants to be a good daughter. She also wants alone time. Sometimes Diana feels pulled between her lives—the one she has in high school and the many others outside it. Everyone wants a part of her. Everyone wants her to do something, be something, be somebody. It takes a lot of effort to navigate between all these pressures.

Over the summer Diana was a lifeguard for the Chicago Park Service. Now she swims on the Payton swim team. She's not the fastest swimmer, but being in the pool is one of the few times she has to herself. As she walks through the hallway to her next class, she says, "You can actually think when you're in the water."

The halls are filled with hugging! In the first week of school, the constant hallway sounds of clanging lockers and squeaking sneakers are punctuated by little explosions: a shriek of recognition, two students throwing their arms wide from a distance of fifteen feet, a quickening shuffle, hug!

Boys do the serious back-pounding version, girls do the delicate lean with one foot raised backward. Boy-on-girl is a side-to-side rocking (the length of which is being exploited by certain boys). But hugs are an opportunity to reconnect with old friends, and size up new ones.

"You're back!"

"I *am!*"

Hallways also become fashion runways. One girl strides down the halls wearing a red T-shirt with a print of a phoenix. Next comes a girl wearing cargo pants so splayed her sneakers are hidden. Then comes a student in a tight T-shirt whose contours make it difficult to read *Everyone Loves an Italian Girl*. With each shirt, the boys standing next to the lockers pretend not to notice how the shirt treats the wearer's breasts.

Boys' shirts don't highlight breasts. The boys saunter down the hallways in frayed T-shirts from Abercrombie & Fitch, or T-shirts embellished with slogans: GEORGE BUSH DOESN'T CARE ABOUT BLACK PEOPLE; appetite for destruction; *War is Costly. Peace is Priceless.*

Finally, shoes. Stripy Adidas, retro Pumas, bright white Dwyane Wade Converse high-tops, Hush Puppies, Uggs, sandals with flowery straps, clogs. Everything you need to know about a student can be told by what is on her feet. A student is her shoes; her shoes are her.

Aisha Kamillah Shaikh sits alone in the library with her Pumas off, right foot tucked underneath her. She has eyes the color of espresso, a petite nose, and coiled dark hair that cascades over her neck and the two necklaces she's wearing: one reads *Allah* in Arabic, the other has a prayer for family and protection.

Aisha is the only transfer in Payton's senior class. She doesn't know anyone here. Her family moved to Chicago last month. Both her parents are engineers and their work moves the family around the world. Last year they were in Florida, the three years before that they lived in Cairo.

The Shaikhs have moved so often that Aisha's father gave each of the children an easily packable box called *The Important Box* in which to keep their favorite possessions. Aisha's *Important Box* has always been filled with toys.

Payton is the first school Aisha has attended where not one girl wears a *hijab*. She doesn't wear one either. Her father is Pakistani. Her mother is Colombian. She has one older brother, two younger sisters. The youngest sister drinks coffee, like her mother. Aisha drinks tea, like her father. The middle sister drinks Vitaminwater and no one in the family can figure out what is up with that.

When Aisha mentions this, she laughs. Her laugh is biting and sharp. She says she inherited her father's sense of humor along with his preference for tea. Her mother, Aisha says, is not funny *at all*. She never got a sense of humor because she left Colombia before she could get one in Spanish, and came to America after she could get one in English, leaving her appreciation for laughter drifting in the stratosphere somewhere above Mexico.

Aisha chuckles, switches her foot from one side to the other, and looks around the library. Book-shelves line three of the library walls, windows fill the other. In the center of the room, students hunch at wood tables over textbooks, or inside carrels staring at computer screens.

Aisha is used to being an outsider. She's used to being alone, used to starting over. She's done this before, she'll do it again. She's just passing through. It's only a year, after all.

Aisha doesn't think she will meet anybody at Payton. With a resigned shrug she says, "There's no incentive to make friends."

On a dirt field a block away from Payton, the J.V. football team is playing its first game of the year and getting demolished. The team they're playing is enormous. They're treating the Grizzlies like cubs. For a high school named after a football player whose nickname was "Sweetness," the Payton J.V. is anything but. Their nickname could be "Sourness," or "Pummeledintothedirtness."

The spectators on the sidelines suffer with the players, wincing with each hit: *"Ouch." "Ooof." "Oh, boy."* When the other team's running back rumbles seventy yards for a touchdown, leaving a crumpled trail of Payton players in his wake, a woman on the sideline says, "It's all right, they'll learn."

The man next to her says, "Yeah, they'll learn how to get run over."

The only ones who seem to be enjoying themselves are members of the Payton varsity, taking a break from their practice. They're standing behind the J.V. and giving advice: "Wrap up!" "Hit!" "Run!" The act of giving advice is proof that they have *arrived,* and this is something to be savored, sweetness itself.

The excitement of the first weeks of school has ebbed, and weariness seeps in. Yawning becomes viral. A boy yawns in class, then infects the girl next to him, who infects the boy next to her, and so on. The yawn continues until it hits an obstacle (a student whose eyes are closed, an empty seat, the teacher), and ricochets back the way it came, back to the boy who started it. The yawn resembles a wave making its way around a stadium.

Struggling out of his class today is Zef Calaveras. Blond bangs hang over Zef's sleepy eyes. A black T-shirt with a skull-and-crossbones hangs on his chest. His skin is the color of flour. Rubber bands wrap around his wrists, headphones around his neck, an iPod from his belt. As he takes a seat on a bench under the stairs in the

atrium, he sort of rattles. Zef's a junior, though already one with a reputation, at least according to Zef. As he slouches into the bench, he mumbles, "Everyone at this school knows I'm a bit odd."

Despite Zef's self-described oddness, he is the object of attention. He's a boy who, just by sitting there, other students approach (it doesn't hurt that he is pale and good-looking in a '70s punk rocker sort of way). In fact, he's always getting interrupted. Other kids like saying hello to Zef. Zef doesn't mind saying hello back. When he waves, he uses his entire arm, as if he's lovingly waxing the hood of a vintage car.

"What up, *Sumner!*"

"*Hey,* Josh Lipinski!"

Over the summer Zef was in a band called Big Roy and the Radio Flyers. But Big Roy started playing "crappy pop punk," so Zef quit. Now he plays by himself late at night. His room is "kinda messy." There's clutter on every surface, posters all over the walls: a transit map he took from a Chicago subway car, a periodic table of the elements, a poster with a giant pistachio nut that some girl gave to him. His window looks out at a brick wall.

Zef stays in his room, playing on his computer and listening to bands like The Strokes or The Killers until early morning. Consequently, the sleepy eyes. His late nights have made for late mornings and a bunch of tardies. He's been dozing during his classes.

"Sumner, what is *up!*"

What is up is music, because Zef is at his most awake during the early-morning jam sessions where he can arrange everything on his computer: drums, base, vocals. Zef is his own band.

"It's *ridiculous*. I've got myself on my iPod," he says, patting his belt. If someone wants to listen to him as they walk past, they can.

There are no boundaries on the floor of the atrium, but that doesn't mean they do not exist. The cool white students sit on the benches outside the boys' bathroom. The boys in this group wear trucker hats (taken off quick when security approaches), bent so vertically the lids look like the top half of exaggeratingly pouty lips. The girls have bodies in whose exhibition they are not unconfident.

Straddling the benches on

the other side of the atrium are the cool black students, wearing baggy hoodies and retro jerseys and baggy jeans (pulled up quick when security approaches). Next to them, the cool Latina students lie on benches in rolled-down sweatpants and designer jeans and tight white tank tops.

Some groups in the atrium segregate by interest: the arty girls who gather under the stairs, where they lie with their heads in their friends' laps and braid each other's hair and knit scarves; the smallish boys who circle the five Ping-Pong tables at the west end of the atrium; the dance girls who practice their routines against the lockers.

Some students don't belong to any group: the boy with the beard, the boy who is bald (not the same boy). The girl with the gap in her teeth an iPod Mini could slide through. The boy with the roller backpack who sits in front of the library, clipping articles out of newspapers and pasting them in a binder.

And then there are students who don't even belong to the school, seemingly floating above the rest of the student body. Like the pretty blond girl in the flippy skirt heading toward the front door in the middle of the day, the girl who makes all the boys' heads swivel.

Anthony Johnson Jr. sits in the cafeteria at a table full of girls. Everyone is laughing, and Anthony is laughing louder than everyone.

Anthony is a junior, an African American boy with bug eyes and a wispy mustache. He has a small head, which is now sticking out of the fuzzy collar of his large green winter jacket. The green jacket makes Anthony look like a turtle hauled up on a beach. Sometimes his head pokes out of his shell and he nibbles a french fry.

Notwithstanding Anthony's winter jacket, it's warm in the cafeteria. Not warm, really, but humid with pore-clogging *friedness*. There are five small windows with no view. Banners for colleges like Notre Dame, Northern Illinois, and Duke circle the top of the cafeteria walls (college is literally hanging over the students' heads). Around the fifty or so tables, students sit according to their race, eating chicken patties. While lunches are given names like *Incredibles,* no amount of wordplay can disguise what the food really is: not so edible.

Consequently there are students who never come to the cafeteria. And then there are those like Anthony who never leave. He always sits in the same seat, back against the far wall. He likes this seat because he can keep everything in front of him. He can clown around, tell jokes, be loud, and "Ain't nobody behind you."

Classes melt away, schoolwork melts away, things he should do but doesn't do melt away. The cafeteria is an island from the rest of school. An island full of girls.

One period later, Anthony is still here.

With the last bell, students pour out the front door: boys carrying skateboards, girls carrying cello cases, blind students tapping their canes, boys in form-fitting 16-Inch softball team uniforms, girls in striped knee-high socks, boys with do-rags under oversized hats, cheerleaders with pom-poms.

As different as the students are, they all do the same thing once they get outside. Ten feet from the door, they stop, take off their IDs and put them in their backpacks, and flip open a cell phone.

Today is Spirit Day. The girls from the cheerleaders and

pom squad have gathered at the front of the school for a rally. As they kick their legs and shake their butts and shout into a megaphone, their cheers make it difficult for other students, as they head out the door with their hands over their ears, to hear their cell phone conversations.

We're headed to the top!
We're not hard to spot!
Walter Payton Grizzlies
Can't be stopped!

OCTOBER

Daniel Patton, senior class president, is waiting outside the guidance counselor's office. He's here for a meeting. He's absentmindedly flipping through a textbook, nodding at classmates who walk past. He says he is studying, though he is not.

"What's going on, Mister President?!" hoots a girl in snug jeans as she sashays past, flashing Daniel a brilliant smile. Daniel smiles back and nods.

What's going on is college applications. Daniel has been writing his personal statement, trying to represent his whole life in just a few lines. It's daunting.

Daniel has lived in the same house since he was a baby. He shares the second floor with his grandmother. His parents live downstairs. Daniel grew up doing normal kid stuff: hanging out, playing ball, running around the neighborhood until the streetlights came on. When he started grade school, his mother enrolled him in academic magnet schools, and soon the other kids in the neighborhood would point at Daniel and say *He's the smart kid*. As his education progressed, he was accepted by better and better public schools in the city, and began to leave his neighborhood behind.

One of the few things that upsets Daniel is when people make the comment that he is articulate, as if that's surprising for someone who is black. He finds it patronizing. But, as a black student who has done well, Daniel also feels like a role model for his community. He feels roots to the neighborhood along with dreams of moving beyond it. Sometimes Daniel just wants to look after Daniel.

He has always been good at moving himself into favorable positions. During his freshman year at Payton, he made himself indispensable by working in the principal's office. He started talking with the guidance counselor about his college plans during his sophomore year.

One of Daniel's essays mentions Illinois senator and rising political star Barack Obama. Obama is one of Daniel's heroes. Not only for his oratory and politics, but for his story. A young African American who went to Columbia and Harvard Law School. A young African American who used connections to get opportunities that led to better connections and more opportunities. To that end, Daniel has been trying to get his essay into the hands of someone he met who is a Harvard trustee, for some feedback.

If Daniel is accepted at Harvard he will attend Harvard. Some of Daniel's teachers say he can write his own ticket. He is also applying to Princeton, Yale, Penn, Duke, Northwestern, Carleton, Michigan, and the University of Illinois. He worries about Harvard's financial aid, though, and his parents would prefer that he go to a college where he would get a better deal.

"I'm not going to *not* go to Harvard just because I can't afford it," he says, crossing his long fingers. "I'm an optimistic person."

Money is often on Daniel's mind. So he sells shoes.

Daniel works in the shoe department at the Nordstrom downtown, selling kids' shoes. Over the summer he sold about twenty-five thousand dollars worth of shoes. He works on commission. On a good day, if he sells a thousand dollars of shoes, that's a couple hundred dollars. Daniel won't sell enough shoes to pay his way through college, but the money helps with application fees, and his own shoes.

He is wearing black leather wingtips today, and a blue suit. He frequently dresses up for student council meetings, committee meetings, other functions. Last week Daniel bought a new jacket, and his class ring. He needs to sell more shoes.

"I have bad spending habits," he says, a sheepish smile creeping over his face. But clothes, like connections, are an investment. If you're going to be the man, you need to look like the man. Looking the man, knowing the man, *being* the man: It's all part of the same package that will let Daniel make his dreams a reality.

The door opens, and the white-haired guidance counselor ushers Daniel inside with a smile and an open arm.

"Lizzie's in *everything*," whispers a spectacled girl into her friend's shoulder. They're walking around the tables in the atrium that have been set up for the school fair, checking out which students have signed up for which club. As of fourth period, here are the numbers:

Student Government: 14
Chess Club: 5
Gay Straight Alliance: 6
African American Club: 10
PLAYA (Payton Latin American Youth Alliance): 8
Asian American Club: 5
Movie Club: 12
Anime and Japanese Culture Club: 12
Payton Players Drama: 23
Animal Rights: 1
Model U.N.: 0
International Club: 25

The International Club's popularity may have something to do with its mission statement:

To enhance the ability to thwart a diverse culture from inhibiting you to complete an overwhelming understanding within this earthly environment while expanding a knowledge including a varied experience.

"What does *that* mean?" says the girl with the glasses.

"No clue," says her friend. "Let's sign up!"

Emily Harris, girls' soccer captain, has goals beyond soccer. She has goals for life. She's got it planned out. She's applying early to Yale. She will get in. After Yale she will work as a consultant, then attend business school at the University of Chicago. Then she will run a company.

"I've always liked that sort of thing, corporations," she says, striding through the hallways after lunch. Emily is wearing jeans and a gray sweatshirt with PAYTON on the chest, her hair pulled tight in its ponytail. Eyes steady, she explains, "I just want to make a lot of money."

This is not entirely true, as Emily also says that her ultimate goal is power.

Emily often plays with her words, pausing to gauge their effect on whomever she's talking with. It's sometimes a question how seriously to take her, especially when she follows whatever she says with her big goalscoring grin.

Emily lives down in Hyde Park, in a red brick

house with a tall chimney on a shaded street near the University of Chicago. Her bedroom is filled with soccer trophies and soccer medals. Out her window she has a view of her backyard, which has a pond and a fountain. On her wall is a painting of an evergreen tree in winter, which Emily bought at a local art fair after saving her allowance when she was young.

Emily's father is a lawyer, her mother a school principal. Her parents divorced when she was in the sixth grade. They remain friends, and the family often gathers for dinners and soccer games. Emily lives with her mother, but is close with both parents. She's the oldest of three sisters. Being the oldest has always made her responsible.

Emily feels responsible for many things in her life. She feels responsible for her studies, for getting straight A's (almost). She feels responsible for helping friends with their homework (which takes longer than her own homework). She feels responsible for acing her college boards, for writing a smart college application essay (intelligent design: wrong).

Mostly, Emily feels responsibility to herself. She just has high expectations. But she doesn't worry much. Emily has little patience for those who worry. Emotions are a sign of weakness, and best kept in check. Emily says her soccer coach at Payton doesn't like it when girls on the team get weepy. A strong exterior is best.

There are few cracks in Emily's exterior. She doesn't trust people easily, doesn't let them in. But then, in the smallest of openings, she admits something: She has a crush on a boy. She hasn't mentioned it to anyone, and hasn't done anything about it. She changes the subject. Her coach was right. Never show weakness.

The first brisk day of fall. Fog wreaths the top of the Sears Tower to the south of school. Passing trains on the "L" sound muffled. As students enter the front door many wear sweatshirts.

Maya Boudreau, the actor with the girl-next-door looks, sits in her English class wearing a long-sleeved Anthropologie shirt and an old pair of jeans. Around her neck is a pastel-flowered scarf. She's fidgeting as usual.

The class is reading *Huck Finn* and discussing race. Ms. Murphy, the teacher, walks around the circle of chairs, trying hard to lure the students into a discussion. Ms. Murphy has a scar above her left eye (courtesy of some sibling roughhousing when she was four). The curve of the scar runs parallel to her eyebrow, giving her face an extra attentiveness. But despite her scar, and her encouragement, the subject of race remains too fraught for the students to say much about, here in Chicago, let alone in America.

Maya watches Ms. Murphy and her classmates struggle, smoothing her hands as if she were washing them. It makes her appear nervous.

Maya is not acting this fall. She's focusing on her applications. She's applying to the theater programs at Northwestern, NYU, and UCLA. She's also applying to Stanford, which she feels is a long shot despite her good grades. Maya will also be directing one of the five student-directed plays this fall, but that is less important than figuring out where she will be next year, which school will let her become what she has always dreamed of becoming: an actor.

When Maya acts, she is not nervous. Her fidgeting disappears.

"It's the most relaxing thing ever. *Ever,*" she says. In the many roles she's had, from those in *The Seagull* to *Caucasian Chalk Circle,* Maya has a certain stage presence. Even playing the weird strung-out characters she prefers, she has an uncanny calmness. Eyes gravitate to her. It's as if she's not acting.

Ms. Murphy says Maya writes like a dream. Ms. Murphy also says that Maya is the girl Ms. Murphy would have wanted to be in high school. An actor, a writer, someone smart *and* pretty. Maya invites this sort of admiration, and yet this is the same girl who, sitting in class now, has just put a sizable chunk of her hair into her mouth and is chewing it.

Maya's two older sisters often ask her why she doesn't have a boyfriend. Her friends from Bourbonnais, the small town in Illinois where she grew up, wonder the same thing. All her friends in Bourbonnais have boyfriends. They all go with their boyfriends to their high school dances. Maya tells them that in Chicago, things are different. It's a cultural thing. Here, students go to parties and hook up.

In any case, the differences don't matter to Maya. She doesn't like going to parties, or to dances. She'd rather go to a play.

In two months, Maya will turn eighteen. Despite the prodding from her Bourbonnais friends and her sisters, she doesn't want a boyfriend. Not one at Payton anyway. The boys at Payton are "always *there*." Like the two good-looking shaggy-haired boys sitting on either side of her, she's with them all the time. They're just friends. They hold no attraction for her.

"I've gone through them all," she says, "in my head."

A teacher hops onto a bench in the atrium and starts shouting instructions. *No* sunglasses, *no* gum, *no* iPods, *no* pagers. Cell phones, if they are brought, *must be turned off.*

Some English classes are taking a field trip to Steppenwolf Theatre. After the buses drop everyone off at the theater, the students are herded to their seats. A Steppenwolf representative comes onstage and reiterates what is not allowed. Don't do this, don't do that. Cell phones, of course, *must be turned off.*

The lights go down, the play begins: Athol Fugard's *"Master Harold" . . . and the Boys.* The performance proceeds with all the professionalism and attention one would expect of one of the country's best theaters, and then, right in the middle of the climactic scene, from the back of the theater, *brreeeiinnngg.* A cell phone. No way. The students swivel their heads to see who could be so incredibly dumb. Somebody is in *big* trouble. Well, no. Jumping out of his seat and out the theater door to answer his cell phone is K. Todd Freeman, the play's middle-aged director.

Diana Martinez and Sandra are best friends. Suki used to be their best friend too. Last year it was the three of them, inseparable.

Diana, Sandra, Suki. They hung out during school, they went shopping after school, and at night they talked on the phone for hours. Sometimes they'd coordinate and come to school the following day in matching outfits.

But this year, something happened between Suki and the other two, and Diana is not sure what.

"It's not like she told my secret or anything, it's not like I told hers," she says quietly as she shuffles through the halls, her voice just audible over the constant slamming lockers, scuffing sneakers, and flushing toilets. Diana ignores the noise and talks about what may have caused the rift.

Maybe it had something to do with junior prom. Suki kissed a boy and didn't tell Diana and Sandra. Diana made fun of the boy in front of Suki. Feelings were hurt.

Or maybe it had something to do with the distances between where they live. Suki lives in Evanston, a suburb north of the city. It took an hour for Diana to drive there from her home on the West Side, and soon after arriving she'd have to turn around and drive back. Chicago is wide and flat, and where you live means something.

Or maybe it had to do with race. Suki has been hanging out with white and Asian friends. Suki is half-white, half-

Asian. Sandra is half-white, half-black. Diana is all Latina.

And maybe it's just something that cannot be explained. In life, things happen. Diana believes people are going to do what they are going to do. You can't make someone into something they're not.

Diana has bigger worries. Her older brother moved back home. He had been living with his wife and baby boy at his in-laws', but things didn't work out. Now he's around the Martinez house all the time. His friends are calling at two in the morning and he can't afford a cell phone. Along with her sisters, he's always telling Diana what to do. It's been stressful.

The stress makes her look forward to swim practice even more. Every afternoon, fifty laps that keep her sane. Two hours that belong to her alone, that allow her to think, to arrange and rearrange the various parts of her life.

"It's relaxful. I just think about *everything*," she says, then pauses. "I talk to myself a lot."

Each morning, students gather in homeroom advisory for ten minutes of unintelligible announcements from the principal. Something about a band concert, something about homecoming. The students are supposed to listen. No one does.

A teacher tries to hush her students: "Listen to the announcement!"

A student responds: "I'm listening, with one ear!"

It's homecoming week, and the walls and lockers of the high school have been plastered with orange construction paper, handmade signs reading *Payton Pride*. Football players strut through the halls in their jerseys. Payton recently adopted the Chicago Bears logo and changed their mascot to the Grizzlies, though the previous name of Navigators remains on the team's uniform. This improvisational quality extends to Payton's stadium. They don't have their own, and borrow that of nearby high school Lane Tech's. Homecoming is not at home.

Saturday breaks clear and bright. Lane Tech's stadium is directly in O'Hare Airport's flight path, and planes fly low overhead, their silver sides glinting in the sun. Joining the planes are V's of geese flying so close to the field that a punt could hit them.

Payton is punting a lot today. The varsity Grizzlies aren't enjoying themselves as much as they were earlier in the season when watching the J.V. get pummeled. But no one is really watching. The real game is in the stands, where students are looking behind them, talking on cell phones, letting friends know where they are.

"Where am *I* at? Where *you* at?" shouts one boy into his phone. Three girls with painted bear paw prints on their cheeks walk past. He waves and gives them air kisses, then keeps scanning for his friends.

On the field, the cheerleaders and pom squad run through their cheers, but mostly stand with their hands in the small of their backs, looking up into the crowd. They don't have cell phones and it looks like they want them. The stands are bustling with planning for that evening.

"What you doing later?"

"We get a touchdown yet?"

"How much more time is left?"

"I put on weight during Ramadan because I eat all night!" says Aisha Kamillah Shaikh with a laugh. She wakes at four in the morning and drinks a glass of water. Then daybreak, and no eating or drinking. After school she goes home and naps until the sun sets. Then she gets up, does her homework, and eats everything in the house.

When Aisha's at school, it is easier to avoid food. Her lunch period is third period, so early she wouldn't eat anyway. She doesn't like the cafeteria either. Too bright, too exposed, with its harsh lighting and clamoring tables of cliques. Aisha prefers the library, ensconced in her carrel. A warm place, a place where she can take off her shoes.

Aisha scratches her foot and explains how her family treats Ramadan.

"The point is not to starve," she says, "but to make yourself appreciate."

Aisha sometimes feels guilty about not being a better Muslim. She doesn't wear a headscarf, she has an occasional drink. Her father isn't traditional—he allows wine during dinner—and has never believed their faith should be a burden. Her parents didn't make Aisha fast on the day she took her ACT test.

The Shaikhs have found a mosque in Chicago that they like, though Aisha finds it odd to pray indoors. In Cairo, everyone prayed in the street. It's also odd that the imam speaks in English (he's African American), and makes jokes. In other mosques, the imams rant in Arabic, which drives Aisha away.

Aisha finds humor in almost anything ("Things that aren't funny, I find something to laugh about!" she says). The odder the better. Cultural references that initially bypass her, once she figures them out, are hilarious. It's a way of seeing America from an angle.

Last week Aisha flew to California to visit her older brother. He's a freshman at Harvey Mudd, one of the Claremont colleges. She liked his roommates, who were nerdy and smart.

Aisha wants to study political science when she goes to college, maybe attend law school afterward. Her Pakistani grandfather thinks Aisha should go to college in California so she can live with her brother, and get a few advanced degrees to enhance her marriage prospects. In an apparent contradiction, her grandfather also thinks she should marry at eighteen (she's seventeen now). He's coming to visit next month.

Aisha won't do something just because someone tells her. She's stubborn that way. Maybe she won't go to California, just to prove a point. Maybe she'll go to art school.

Aisha loves art. There's a portfolio class at Payton she's already enjoying. Ever since she can remember, she's kept sketchbooks filled with little drawings and snippets of paper. She has ones from China, where the Shaikhs lived when she was eight. Aisha wants to hang some of her paintings on the walls of the family's new Lincoln Park condominium. They're pretty bare right now. The floors, however, are covered in pillows and rugs. In the master bedroom, which Aisha shares with her little sister, there's a huge and intricate Pakistani rug, which, depending on the perspective it is looked at, completely changes color from dark to light.

Aisha has less energy for her art when she's fasting, less energy for anything. Sometimes it's hard to concentrate, to study, especially when the students in the next library carrel are munching on smuggled bars of candy. But *Eid ul-Fitr* is coming up, and the end of her fast. She can't wait to snack, to be able to eat whatever she wants whenever she wants. She's been dreaming of Reese's Pieces, and a hot dog with everything (except the pickles).

Mr. Dyson, a physics teacher at Payton, has a smooth shaved head the color of a chestnut. A football player in college, he seems to compensate for his imposing size and demeanor by speaking in an especially kind and patient manner. But Mr. Dyson is not himself today. Today he is *Bonginkosi*. It's Thursday—the day at Payton where students take seminars as varied as *The Israeli-Palestinian Conflict* and *Intro on B-boying*. This means that Mr. Dyson/*Bonginkosi* is teaching Zulu.

Eyes popping like Ping-Pong balls, gold hoop earring shaking, he circles the room and slaps the surface of the tables and shouts *"Yebo!"* As he strides past the black-and-white poster of Einstein that, in a calmer moment, he hung on his classroom door, he is a wild man. The students stare at him wide-eyed. All the students, that is, except for Zef Calaveras, head resting comfortably on his desk, fast asleep.

——

A few days later, Zef is awake. He's slumping on his bench under the atrium stairs. He yawns. He was late to school again. It's becoming a problem. He has nine tardies already this year, which, he says, is "ridiculous."

Zef flips his bangs out of his eyes and leans back. If he leaned more he'd be flat. Two teachers walk past and ask where he was this morning. He mumbles something in response. Then, to no one in particular: "It sucks starting your day with lunch."

Last night, Zef couldn't fall asleep. After walking the family dogs, he ate an entire pizza. Then he spent a couple hours laying down tracks on his computer. He still couldn't settle down. Even his bed didn't help. Zef has an electric remote-control bed he got from his grandmother, which allows him to raise his feet or his head, depending on the mood. The bed even vibrates, for added relaxation and comfort. Finally, at four in the morning, Zef slept. He says he has insomnia.

Coffee helps. On Zef's drive to school today he stopped at Starbucks and got a six shot, half-decaf, no water, iced venti Americano, which, he says, "gets you up very well." He's nursing the dregs now.

"Usually when I leave school at the end of the day, I'm awake by then."

Zef pauses to scratch his armpit.

"I should run on Pacific Coast Time!"

His joking aside, Zef doesn't like falling asleep in class. He'll be sitting in biology and dimly become aware that he physically cannot keep his eyes open. It feels like some great weight pushing down on him. Then he sleeps, and doesn't dream. It's not restful. And when the teacher wakes him, he finds he's often slept through most of class. Sleeping is hurting his schoolwork.

Zef sees a group of students approaching. They're preppy, put-together. When Zef notices students like these he thinks, *I am not like these people.* The students wave at Zef. Zef waves back. They keep walking. Zef also knows that students like these think he's cool, maybe because he's the guy who falls asleep in class.

A girl in a wheelchair speeds past. Zef waves. "Rolling *thunder!*"

The friend brakes and they talk. She keeps rolling. Two pretty girls approach, hands resting on their hips. From his prone position, Zef cocks his head sideways, smiling up at the girls through the strands of his hair, looking like a cat under a bird feeder. They gossip, smile broadly, leave. Zef takes a pull

from his Americano and drums out a beat on his leg.

"Today's shaping up to be *all right*." He chuckles. "Though, I forgot to do my homework."

The homecoming dance is *on*. Girls totter in first wearing high heels, hair straightened or poofed. Boys in jackets follow the girls. Daniel Patton slips through the front door wearing a stylish gray suit. The atrium fills with students exclaiming how hot they all look.

The lights go down, the music goes up. Girls hit the floor first, followed by the boys. Some dancers are unsure, with moves like al dente spaghetti. Others are sure.

Gwen Stefani's hit "Hollaback Girl" turns on and the girls and boys start bouncing. The dance floor takes on the appearance of a popcorn popper. Out of the popper come three girls, yanking up their fronts, heading to the bathroom. In goes a boy and girl, grinding against each other, unintentionally pinning a small boy beneath them.

Out comes a girl with her breasts spilling out of her dress, dragged by a chaperone who reprimands her for dancing too sexily. Around goes the rumor that the after-party will be at a nearby penthouse (five dollars for seniors, seven for juniors, fifteen for freshman). Out comes an arguing couple. In goes the arguing couple. Out pops a girl, dress straps off-kilter, shouting, *"Agua!"*

There is one girl in the middle of the floor dancing by herself. She's blond and willowy. She's wearing a slinky backless green dress. Unlike the other girls it doesn't seem as if she's performing. Boys stare at her, and give her space. She's the best dancer here.

After a few sweaty hours, the music skitters to a halt. The Homecoming King is announced and given a velvet crown to a chorus of squeals. Balloons fly up, streamers fall down, and packs of boys, arms wide and fingers pointing, shout the years of their graduating class at each other: "Oh-*eight!*" "Oh-*seven!*" "Oh-*six!*"

Then, *poof,* on go the lights, and in that unconsummated glare everyone picks up their heels and slings their jackets over their shoulders and heads back to the front door.

The solitary dancer in the backless green dress? Her name is Anais Blake. She's a senior, a ballet dancer. Every day after her third-period precalculus class, Anais leaves school and walks three blocks to the Ruth Page Center for the Arts. She takes classes there in the studio, returning to Payton two hours later. Sometimes it seems to Anais that she's living two lives.

Anais has a sweet oval face and straight blond hair the color of vanilla ice cream. She has the body of, well, a dancer. Even when she's not moving—listening to her dance instructor tell anecdotes about how it was back in Russia—she appears graceful. She stands out, just like she did at the homecoming dance. It's hard not to stand out when you are regularly the prettiest girl in a room.

When Anais was two, her mother brought her to a dance performance, and afterward Anais ran up on stage and began jumping around. Dance classes soon followed, with ballet classes starting when she was seven. For as long as Anais can remember, dancing has been her life: classes each day, performances each weekend, camp each summer. This last summer she went to dance camp in New York, at Juilliard.

After high school Anais wants to go either to Juilliard, or to the renowned ballet conservatory at Indiana University. Like any serious dancer, her dream is to join a professional company someday, though that may be a leap now. Leaping has always been Anais's favorite thing.

Walking from the studio back to school a few days after the homecoming dance, Anais unwraps the Kit Kat chocolate bar she grabbed from the jar outside the studio and talks about her dance friends and her high school friends. The differences stress her out.

Dance friends can be intense, often thinking only about dance. Anais feels comfortable with them, though, especially after a performance. They've experienced the same high together, and can reflect in its glow (she sometimes finds it hard to even talk after dancing). Dancers are crazy, but at least it's a craziness they share. She knows she's obsessed with dance. All good dancers are.

Anais's high school friends don't understand. They ask her to go out and are hurt when she says no. Anais knows she needs rest, knows she can't stay out late drinking.

Her body is an instrument that must be kept in good shape. She feels guilty for not being a better friend, but angry that her friends don't empathize more. One of the few who does is Maya Boudreau. Maya is one of Anais's best friends. As a performer, Maya understands what Anais goes through. Others do not.

"They don't know what I do. Not really," Anais says, biting into her Kit Kat bar and frowning.

She has her feet in two worlds. Dance and school. Maintaining balance between the two requires some flexibility, a certain grace. When she stops at the traffic light a block from Payton her feet are turned out perfectly.

The Chicago White Sox are in the World Series. Sox fever has infected Payton. The high school is plastered with big black-and-white signs, lettered GO WHITE SOX in the windows facing the "L." A clothesline across the atrium is hung with white socks.

As if to celebrate the team, the skinny kid with the big ears in English is flipping his pencil particularly high today, like a cheerleader's baton, even though he's sitting next to Ms. Murphy. As class starts, the skinny kid catches every flip, though as his pencil rises higher toward the ceiling, defying gravity and common sense, it asks a series of increasingly interesting questions: How high can the pencil go, how much time before Ms. Murphy says something, how long can this last? About one minute. With a thud, the pencil falls directly into Ms. Murphy's open book.

Anthony Johnson Jr., the boy who never leaves the cafeteria, is sitting in his turtle shell jacket against the back wall of the room. He's talking with a girl. He is supposed to be in class.

Anthony's favorite word is *situation,* as in, "There was a situation with me and The Girl." The Girl he's referring to is sitting across from him now, staring at him. As he starts to explain the situation, The Girl picks up her tray without a word and leaves. Anthony watches her go. Last year, The Girl was the girlfriend. Over the summer, things changed.

"There was a certain situation in July, know what I'm saying?"

It started with a returned gift, a White Sox hat one size too big. Then Anthony got angry when another boy started talking to The Girl too much. Then they broke up. And though Anthony and The Girl no longer are going out, he holds out the hope that they may. They're still best friends, he says. Last

weekend he talked with her from eight in the evening until three in the morning.

"I can't *not* talk to her," he says, looking up at the ceiling.

Anthony's situation with The Girl affects *everything*. It's the air he breathes. If it weren't for The Girl, he wouldn't come to school. He's not doing well in school as it is. He's failing his classes. Or cutting classes, like right now. Anthony is on academic probation, technically a sophomore, one year behind everyone else.

Phys ed is playing flag football on the field next to the high school. Students hug their elbows on the sidelines to stay warm. Everyone is hoping to play, or hoping they don't have to.

"We need a quarterback. *We need a quarterback,*" shouts one boy with spiky hair. A chubby boy takes a turn, throws an interception, and does not get another turn. At least he got to touch the ball. Girls don't. After half an hour, boys have thrown to boys on every single play. Girls don't get thrown to. They

stay on the sidelines, or run around the field in little ignored circles.

Then, maybe by mistake, a ball *is* thrown to a girl. She catches it, hops to the side to evade one onrushing boy, and then, with a gasp from the sidelines—who knew!—she bursts past the other boys, her ponytail streaming behind her, and slides shyly into the end zone, not knowing what to do with the ball once she gets there.

Her team envelops her in a hug, almost lifting her up. It is a cold overcast morning, but as the girl is escorted to the sidelines, her teammates tousling her hair, the sun actually breaks through the gray.

NOVEMBER

The trees in front of Payton have loosened their grip at the same time. Leaves are everywhere, skittering in whirlwinds, resting on the ground for a moment before lifting into the air again. The blustery weather outside seems to affect the atmosphere inside school. In Ms. Murphy's English class, things are sort of unmoored.

"Everyone look at me and create the illusion of focus!" begs Ms. Murphy in one of her carefully-worded-yet-ignored pleas. Her irony doesn't register. Attention is wandering. Not wandering, more like starring in a movie.

When Maya Boudreau daydreams about New York, she

pictures herself starring in some cool independent *Lost in Translation*–type movie with Kevin Kline. Maya would play the Scarlett Johansson role, the smart ingénue. Kevin Kline would be Bill Murray. The role could be played by other actors of his generation whom she respects (Maya's daydreams are open to suggestion), but her first choice would be Kline. Wes Anderson, whose movies she loves, could direct.

They would film on the streets of New York, in apartments and high-ceilinged lofts. The cast and crew would be professional, passionate. After the day's shoot, they would all go to an off-Broadway show, a late dinner, the night ending at a party in some Soho loft. In Maya's daydreams, more than a few lofts are involved.

As much as this is a daydream, Maya thinks it's plausible. It could happen, with or without Kevin Kline. It's a dream where each angle can be lovingly considered, a daydream she can lose herself in, a dream where a paper ripped from a notebook is the roar of the subway, the crack of knuckles are shoes walking down Broadway, the click of a mechanical pencil is the clink of a wineglass, and the voice of the teacher is the director calling *Action*.

When Ms. Murphy mentions that class may need to come in Saturday morning to watch a five-hour film version of *Hamlet,*

attention is achieved *like that*. It folds the set and packs the bags and gets on a plane back to Chicago, incredulous and breathless.

The entire class scurries back from their individual daydreams. There is complete utter focus on Ms. Murphy's next words. If a flipped pen could hang in the air, it would. She can*not* be serious. She *is* serious. Five minutes later, though, Ms. Murphy relents.

Everyone breathes again. Someone cracks her knuckles, someone rips a piece of paper, and the attention of the room whirls off into another dream, maybe out West, hiking through meadows in the shadow of snow-covered mountains, up into the clouds.

———

"If I get in, I'll probably do some sort of victory . . ." Daniel Patton's voice drifts off and he crosses his fingers. Daniel crosses his fingers often, especially when talking about applying to Harvard.

Daniel is sitting outside the guidance counselor's door again, his lanky frame tilting precipitously backward. If he tilted any farther he'd fall into the counselor's office. Daniel is wearing a gray Italian suit, a blue French tie. He's dressed up for a meeting down at city hall later today. He's not only the president of the Payton senior class, but also the mayor of Chicago in a YMCA youth council program that meets in the city council chambers.

Next week, on the day Daniel finds out whether or not he got in early admission to Harvard, he will be dressed up too.

School, a student council meeting, a meeting at city hall, then selling shoes at Nordstrom. Busy, busy, busy.

The librarian walks past, waves, and says, "Hi, honey!"

He smiles up at her.

Daniel is waiting to fill his guidance counselor in on recent developments, check if there are any extra ways he can make himself appear to be a better candidate for Harvard. He finds the process nerve-racking. It's been testing his normally cool demeanor.

The door opens and the guidance counselor pokes his head out of his office.

"Are you retaking that test?"

"Yes. I'm studying for it."

"No, you're not," says the counselor. They both laugh. Daniel is the type of student that teachers want to take under their arms, that teachers hope will succeed. There are some concerns about Daniel's scores, however. His ACT score is good but not great. He's not getting straight A's, though he is taking difficult AP courses. He has more B's than A's.

But Daniel has all the incalculables. The extra-curriculars, the committees, the meetings, the recommendations, the respect of teachers and classmates. The *bearing*. The ability to convey that he is unfailingly eager and polite. Listening, conferencing, networking.

And all this takes effort.

Sometimes the effort leaves him with less time to study, to crack books as hard as he knows he should.

At the corner of Cermak and Throop on Chicago's South Side, in the shadow of a factory pumping steam into the night sky, is a cavernous brick warehouse indistinguishable from the other warehouses around it except for what is being manufactured inside: soccer players.

Chitown Fútbol. Tuesday night and the place is thumping. On two turf fields, teams of girls in bright uniforms sprint after each other and kick balls off the walls. The warehouse echoes. Parents shout from the stands. In the middle of all this commotion, letting it spin around her, is Emily Harris.

She does not run. She shuffles. With her elbows out, she looks like a cocky duck. Her shuffle actually makes her look like she's moving slower than the other players. But she has the sixth sense of knowing where the ball will be two passes before

it gets there, then shuffles to that spot before everyone else.

As Emily settles the ball she does so gen-
tly, glancing up to see if her teammates are in
the correct position. Emily is constantly thinking. Then two defenders rush her and she
effortlessly slides the ball to one side, letting
them charge past her as if they were bulls, before bending a
perfect pass to an unmarked teammate for an open shot. *Gol.*

At halftime, Emily's team is ahead 8–0. Emily
spends the second half distributing the ball to her
teammates, shouting directions as if the other
team were not there. The other team finds this
particularly frustrating. They may as well be cones.

Emily says her favorite player is Ronaldo, the
Brazilian striker. But she plays more like his
countryman Ronaldhino. They have the same
midfield position, the same creative playmaking, the same
goldish cleats, the same serious face that breaks into a flashy
smile. With her cocoa skin and black ponytail she looks
like she could be Ronaldhino's kid sister.

But unlike Ronaldhino, Emily rarely takes her own shot.

After school, Maya Boudreau's all-female cast shows up in the third-floor rehearsal room. They're yawning. Maya stares at them and says, "Why don't you take a lap around the school? You're *really* low energy!"

The girls stare at her.

"No. *Really*," she replies. "Let's do it!"

Maya leads the girls through the hallways in a gangly jog. They come back panting, and start blocking the play. Maya sits in her director's chair, rolling her right foot.

The role of director comes easily to her. She chews her pencil, occasionally taking it out of her mouth to make notes in the script.

The actors are having some difficulty, and making complaints:

"I don't know the next line!"

"I don't know how to stand!"

"I don't know where to put my arms!"

"I don't know how to hold a baby!"

Maya meets each worry with a calm response:

"Okay, read your script."

"Well, maybe move around."

"At your sides is fine."

"Imagine the baby is a puppy and you're talking to it."

For all their complaining, the girls clearly look up to Maya. In another era, Maya is the type of girl who would teach younger girls how to bake a pie. Here she is teaching them how to act.

And the girls, if unintentionally, are teaching Maya. Making her translate all the advice she's been given over her years of acting, making her explain things she just *knows*. It's a challenge. She has a definite idea of where she wants the play to go, but how do you ask another person to give you something they don't know how to give?

Down the hall from Maya's rehearsal, a meeting of *Paw Prints* has just begun. The newspaper's room is a mess of monitors and printers. On one wall is a white board with a drawing of a chicken.

As the faculty advisor peppers the students with questions about their articles, they stutter in response. The staff is mostly male. Most have unmanaged hair, brown corduroys, pale skin. The few girls of *Paw Prints* are better groomed and more assertive, possibly because here they have found boys over whom they can assert themselves.

Two *Paw Prints* boys are not like the others. They're the two shaggy-haired boys from Maya's English class. The larger one is named Ben. The smaller one is named Andy. Their shaggy hair does not hide their good looks. If anything, it adds to it. As the rest of the *Paw Prints* staff hunches at their computers, Ben and Andy straddle chairs and throw ideas back and forth at each other, casually jawing. They're seniors, best of friends. They hang out with each other so much that classmates often refer to them by one name: Ben&Andy.

On the wall behind Ben&Andy is a poster with this quotation: "A writer is a person for whom writing is more difficult than it is for other people," words of advice that don't seem to apply to them.

Diana Martinez got a job. A friend's mother runs a day-care center and Diana started working there after school. The swim team's season just finished, and the time Diana used to spend in the pool is now spent taking care of toddlers. The job doesn't fit her. She doesn't like taking care of other people, especially little people. All the crying, all the aggravation of trying to get them to sleep, the *routine*. It's making Diana ill. She's already been home sick four days this month and is falling behind in her classes. She finds she's more tired than when she was swimming, with little energy for homework. And there are things going on at home that she doesn't want to talk about.

Diana looks across the atrium.

Every day this fall, recruiters from colleges as varied as Michigan and MIT have been setting up tables in the atrium to sell their schools. Today's recruiters are from the U.S. Marine Corps. Two Latino boys in crisp khaki shirts and ironed blue pants. They look smaller than the students they're recruiting. They stand, backs straight, trying to hand out free stuff to students who walk past. The students ignore them and gather around the Ping-Pong tables, the *pock-pock-pock* of the games as constant as a ticking clock.

Diana has been thinking about where she will apply to college. She's looking mostly at Midwestern schools: Iowa, Illinois, Loyola, the University of Illinois at Chicago,

DePaul. Colleges that are close to home, but not too close.

She misses swim practice. She misses those fifty laps she had to herself. With her new job, Diana swims only one day a week now, during her Thursday seminar. She would try to swim more, but her best friend Sandra swims with her, and Sandra complains that the chlorine does bad things to her hair. So Diana, to be a good friend, doesn't swim as much.

A slim boy walks through the halls, right arm around a girl. The girl is wearing a huge winter coat, her hooded head buried in the boy's shoulder, her arm slack against his chest. But she has no legs. It takes a moment, as they approach, to see that there is no girl, no *they,* only the coat itself. Winter has come to Chicago.

Aisha has never owned a winter coat. There was never any reason to. Cairo winters and Chicago winters are a little different. So last weekend the Shaikhs drove to the malls outside the city. Aisha bought a long coat with buttons and a shorter jacket with pretty embroidery. She and her middle sister also loaded up on stockings and sweaters. They'll share. They share everything.

The four females in the Shaikh family all have the same-size feet. This exponentially expands Aisha's shoe options. She can wear her mother's dress shoes when she wants, or her sisters' Pumas when she doesn't want to wear her own Pumas, because she loves Pumas and would wear Pumas all the time if she could. Aisha is a little obsessed with Pumas. The only problem with sharing shoes is that her littlest sister doesn't wear socks and, Aisha groans, "She has stinky feet!"

Aisha's Pumas are off now, her stockinged legs folded beneath her in her library carrel. Sitting next to her are a couple of girls from Aisha's art class. They're doing their homework together, occasionally glancing up from their books to ask each other questions. Aisha has become friendly with these girls. It's been nice, but she knows there's a difference between friend*ly* and friend-*ship*. These are not people she hangs out with after school.

Aisha mostly hangs out with her sisters. Over the weekend she went downtown with her middle sister in their new jackets. Their father dropped them off. After looking at the Christmas lights and getting hot chocolate at Marshall Field's, they realized they didn't have enough money for the "L" ride home. Aisha called her father and he picked them up. He wasn't mad. He's protective. And, Aisha says, she's his favorite.

Her father is strict, but Aisha knows how to deal with him (the middle sister clashes with him more). *What he says, goes* doesn't necessarily mean that what he says can't be selectively heard. And, he has a sense of humor. There's only one thing he doesn't have a sense of humor about: The girls are not allowed to date until they leave home.

"If he knew, he'd go crazy!" Aisha says, eyes widening to indicate that she *has* dated and that her father never found out. She doesn't say whether she would take that risk again. No boys at Payton interest her anyway. She looks across the library at some underclassmen horsing around a table.

"The boys here are timid, they don't talk a lot. And the ones who *do* talk, don't stop talking."

She laughs, looks again.

"It's a lot of effort to make friends, and to have a boyfriend I'd have to be friends with them before . . ." She trails off. "I'll probably just wait until college."

Zef Calaveras had quite a weekend. Friday night he got a girlfriend, Saturday morning he got a mixing board, Saturday night he got tested for insomnia, Sunday night he didn't fall asleep until four (which would make that Monday morning), and he slept through his alarm and was late to school, again.

Now he's slumping under the stairs in his black pirate T-shirt, draining his six shot, half-decaf, no water, iced venti Americano.

Working backward, starting with Saturday. Because Zef's sleeplessness had been getting worse, his mother took him to a sleep study center. He was hooked to electrodes, a wire contraption was shoved up his nose, then he was left in an unpleasant room (someone nearby was working a jackhammer) and told to sleep. For eight hours Zef lay there wide-awake.

"It was so *ridiculous!*"

The sleep doctor was exasperated.

"The guy was really *strange*. Though if you had to sit up all Saturday night watching people sleep, *you'd* be sort of strange too."

The upshot is that Zef was pulled from the sleep study program and is hoping a sedative will help him get to sleep, and to school on time.

The new mixing board may not help. Zef's mother is a Buddhist so on Saturday, to celebrate Bodhi Day, she gave him a mixing board. Zef lives with his mother (his parents are in the process of divorcing), in a beige brick two-story on the city's West Side, a block away from Western Avenue and its many blinking used-car dealerships. Since Zef's room is a mess, he may keep the mixing board elsewhere in the house. He dreams about turning a room in the house into a studio. The mixing board has all these cool features he can describe in detail and—

"What up, *Sumner!*"

"Hey, did you do the bio?"

"*What* bio? *Shit.* What was I saying?"

Zef continues describing the mixing board, and the girl-friend. She's cute. She goes to Payton. She's a sophomore. They started hanging out last year in phys ed, then after school in the parking lot, then at her apartment. They were just friends, though he always thought she was sweet. Friday evening they were instant-messaging and that's when they agreed to go out.

So, all things considered, an excellent weekend, whose excellence cannot completely cover over the fact that Zef is getting D's in his classes. He yawns and sips his coffee.

"Have I mentioned that I hate precal?"

—

The Payton student body may be the best Ping-Pong-playing student body in America. From the start of the day until the last bell, the five Ping-Pong tables in the atrium are continually occupied.

There is one player who is better than everyone. He's a freshman, spectacled and Asian, the top of his jutting hair not much higher than the table. But he has all the shots, the swerving serves and funky grips. He even has a fan club of other small boys who circle the table and admire his every move. One of the kids in the club nods at the boy and whispers, "He's the *King* of Ping-Pong."

Anais Blake hurt her ankle. She was dancing in the studio over Thanksgiving break when she felt a sharp pain in her right foot. The pain spread down her arch and up her calf. After class she got a massage, but that didn't help. The following day she tried to dance but had to stop it hurt so bad. Now she's in the library, a place Anais rarely finds herself. A biology textbook lies unopened in front of her.

She's holding an ice pack to her foot. The foot is flushed, its veins pulsing. When Anais removes the ice pack she turns her ankle in circles, looking at it as if it's not part of her, as if it might start talking and reassure her that everything will be okay.

But it is impossible for Anais to separate from her body.

When Anais dances well, it's the most wonderful feeling in the world, the purest feeling, one where her body and soul are working together as one. It's almost as if she were a different person. When she is hurt, this feeling falls apart, and doubt creeps in. So this is more than an ankle sprain.

Anais says bodies do not lie. If her body is hurt, what does that say?

The more Anais looks at her ankle, the more she seems about to cry. The timing could not be worse. Her audition for the ballet conservatory at Indiana is on Friday.

Hanging over the security desk at the front door is a television monitor. The screen flips from weather reports (cold) to upcoming events (Choir Concert, 7:00), to this warning:

Cutting Classes?
Thinking of skipping class?
Don't do it!
You will be found!

Anthony Johnson Jr. ditched school last week. He and The Girl agreed to meet at the McDonald's, but they missed each other. There are a lot of McDonald's around Payton and they went to different McDonald's. The Girl didn't have a cell phone, so Anthony couldn't reach her, but on his way back to Payton there she was walking back to school too, so they took the "L" to Anthony's gray stone house on the West Side and hung out in his room, which was where his father caught him.

"I can't win! I ain't ever cut class without getting caught!" Anthony shouts up at the ceiling, slapping his table in the cafeteria and surprising the kids at the next one over. With that he gets up and heads to class (the class after the class he cut), shuffling down the hall in a slow pigeon-toed gait, disappearing into the student body.

December

At this point in the year, the savvier students have found the dead spots that authority can't reach. The third floor near the windows to talk on cell phones. The carrels in the library farthest from the librarian. The elevator when security walks away from their desk.

The only truly dangerous spot remaining in the high school is the stairway on the second floor as it passes by the band room. That's where the band teacher stands between classes, staring at the students as they walk up, waiting to pounce on those who are late. The band teacher's patience is short, like his sideburns and his pants. Sometimes the traffic on the stairs bottles up and students are slowed down. Today a straggler is caught, an event heralded by some roaring from outside the band room. As the band teacher drives his prey downstairs to the security desk, he shouts, "When a teacher tells you to move, *you move*! Next time this happens, *I write you up*! And I don't need, *your mouth*!"

It's Andy, the smaller half of Ben&Andy. He looks thoroughly annoyed. He's smart and good-looking, he will go to an excellent college. But right now, in the clutches of the band teacher, he's as helpless as a landed fish. That everyone else in the school is getting away with everything makes the indignity doubly wrong.

 "I don't know what I'm doing yet," Maya mutters as she walks toward the cafeteria. She's hugging a metal money box and a wheel of red tickets to her chest. She seems unsure how to proceed.

"I don't know what to do," she mutters again, staring at the folding table outside the cafeteria doors. Two freshman boys with pimples walk by.

"Do you want to go to the play on Friday?" Maya calls to the backs of their heads. The boys turn and smile but keep walking. Another boy passes and doesn't acknowledge her. Maya shakes her head.

"Did you *see* that? He didn't even respond to me. *Argh,* that was so rude." She sticks her tongue into her cheek, and sits down with a thump.

"I'm terrible at this."

Maya opens her money box and starts clucking her tongue. More boys walk past.

Then one friend approaches and buys a ticket. Maya gives a little clap and cries, *"Yay!"* A minute later, another friend and another ticket. Maya hops up and tracks down a boy across the hall. After ten minutes, and a few more sales, she's on a roll.

"Do you want to go to the play on Friday? I think you do!"

The last weeks have been stressful for Maya. Applications are taking up all her time. Getting her essay just right. Maya wrote hers about Bourbonnais, the town in Illinois her family moved from, the place that gave her the small-town look she hasn't entirely lost. She wrote about how everyone there is

74

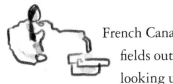 French Canadian, how her house had woods and fields out back where she spent her childhood looking under rocks for worms, how she lived this bucolic life before moving to the big city. There's humor in her essay. But the process behind it has been intimidating.

"I've tried out for plays and gotten rejected," Maya says, fingering one red ticket. "This is different. It's ultimate, *final*. It could be for life."

Maya is faced with this life-changing pressure, and yet her day-to-day worries have a way of intruding. For instance, she may be selling tickets for a play that won't go on. An assistant principal sat in on their rehearsal two days ago and had some issues. Maya's play is about a mother who abandons a newborn baby in a mall crèche. That wasn't the problem. The assistant principal, according to Maya, worried about the message being sent by having a character who slept around.

"They're ridiculous," Maya says, nodding toward the administration offices where the play is being read by someone else in authority to make sure it is "safe."

She bites her lip and frowns and says, not sounding fine, "It'll be fine."

———

The atrium is a stage on which to perform for one's classmates. Every season needs a hit, and this fall it's a play starring the Homecoming King. The play has no words. It starts with the Homecoming King standing in front of his open locker. The Homecoming King's girlfriend lies on the floor beneath him, one leg crawling up the inside of the Homecoming King's thigh. She runs it up and down, hooking it behind the back of his leg, slowly dragging him to her. They sink downward. After twelve minutes they are lying together on the linoleum.

Diana's come to school this morning with straightened hair, swooping and fancy. She had it done over the weekend at the salon (named Diana's Salon) next door to her house. Since Diana's hair gets dry in the cold weather, the woman at Diana's suggested she rub an old avocado into it and—

BOOM!

An explosion rips through the high school. Diana, walking slowly up the atrium stairs, does not flinch. In fact, she barely stops the sentence she's working on to explain: "Oh, *ye-eh-es,* they are doing a science experiment." A chemistry class has been turning plastic bottles into rockets with the help of hydrogen, and shooting them up through the atrium (the height the rocket reaches is the grade: first-floor railing a C, second-floor railing a B, third-floor railing an A). Another explosion rattles the school, but Diana keeps walking to the benches by the windows that overlook the train tracks. As she takes a seat it would seem that very little would rattle her.

Diana's older brother was arrested. Supposedly he threatened some guy in their neighborhood who turned out to be to a police informant. Now her brother is in jail, at Cook County. Bail was set impossibly high. Diana has missed a few days of school going to Cook County to figure out what the family should do. Her mother and father are not confident with English, and it is Diana who handles the translating.

"I've been doing that since I was, like, small," she says. Insurance, credit cards, refinancing—any communication that came through the Martinez house was Diana's to translate. She never liked feeling she might translate a word incorrectly. It worried her to advise her father. It was a job she didn't want, even as she became better at it.

When Diana first saw her brother she yelled at him. How could he be so dumb? How could he hurt his family? Did he stop to think how this would affect his mother, his child? The whole thing makes Diana so angry. She's angry at her sisters too. Why aren't *they* the ones going to the jail to ask questions? They don't go to school. They're sitting around the house.

They've started working at a car wash a few days a week, but mostly they just go to clubs at night. And they always tell Diana what to do. As she mentions this, she throws out both of her hands in frustration as if shooing away mosquitoes.

This incident with her brother is a distraction from her schoolwork. She's not understanding calculus. Her schoolwork is a distraction from her college applications. She's behind in writing her essay. Her job at the day-care center distracts her by itself, and when Diana comes home she is too exhausted to concentrate on anything, let alone write an essay explaining her life. Everything is a distraction from everything else.

The one thing that used to calm her down, she no longer has time to do. She misses swimming, more than ever.

Emily Harris's friends are freaking out. It's Friday, and colleges are posting online who got accepted and who got deferred. Some friends are in tears. Since colleges don't say exactly when they will post, students spend the whole day stressing and crying and logging on to computers.

Emily is in AP physics on a computer. She decides to check too. She's nervous, but she certainly isn't in tears. Mostly she's curious about when the post will be up. Nothing yet. While she is checking, her physics teacher walks up behind her and sees what she's doing. He says, "I know you're worried about college, Emily, but don't be. Any school would be stupid not to take you."

After school, she drives home in her green Honda Civic. Her

laptop is upstairs, so she walks up and logs on, and there on the screen is the Yale Bulldog singing the Yale fight song, which means that she has been accepted.

The Harris household turns into media central. Her mother makes Emily call her grandparents and other relatives, and that night the whole family goes out to a celebratory dinner (steak).

Emily isn't surprised. She's relieved. Relieved that no one had hurt her chances by neglecting to send in some important form. With her grades, her boards, her soccer, she feels she should have gotten in. It was like a penalty shot. She was *supposed* to make it. *Not* making it would be the bigger story. Emily's father was even more confident, so certain Emily would get in that two weeks ago he bought a bottle of champagne. Emily insists that getting into Yale is no big deal. However, in the days afterward as she walks through the hallways of school, receiving congratulations from teachers and students, the grin on her face, and the length of time it stays there, says otherwise.

Under orange and blue banners, the wooden bleachers of the gym fill with students waiting for the girls' first basketball game of the year. The Grizzlies' opponent today is the Latin School, a nearby private school. The Latin team runs onto the court organized by height and weaves around in finely tuned drills. The Payton team stumbles onto the court, backing into each other like cattle in a chute.

At the gym door, there's more trouble getting in. Admission is two dollars. No one wants to pay. Students try to bargain with the security guard.

"What if I watch through the window? How 'bout one-fifty!"

Some of the private school parents are upset.

"*Our* school doesn't charge," gripes a lady in a floor-length fur coat.

"Hey, we're a Chicago public school!" the security guard hoots.

Fur-coat lady shouts to a player on the Latin bench: "Hey, [Unintelligible]. Can I borrow two dollars?" Unintelligible pretends not to hear. The security guy chuckles and waves her inside.

"Two dollars? Are you serious?" says the next parent, rummaging in her purse. "Can you break a hundred?"

The security guy gives her an *are you kidding me* look. She is not, and hands him a crisp Ben Franklin. He pushes the bill away like it's a used napkin and waves her in. He's having a great time.

The game starts. The gym shakes with thumps and squeaks and whistles. One Payton guard, lithe and pony-tailed, is scoring at will. The Latin School can't stop her, so they foul her. She stands at the free-throw line, bouncing the ball, then takes a breath that can be heard from the stands. The gym is as quiet as the library never is. But, as the shot is halfway on its trajectory to the net, a shout comes from the door: "Two *dollars?!*"

Monday mornings are never good, and even worse when your mother forgets to take the toast out of the toaster, sending smoke everywhere, waking you up, making you stumble around with blankets over your head trying to open the windows. All in all, a lousy way to start the week for Zef Calaveras.

"How do you set a toaster on fire?" Zef asks the Toaster Gods from his spot under the stairs. He coughs.

"I have allergies. I can't breathe. And, I smell."

It's true. Friends approach and hug Zef and say, "What's *that?*"

There's nothing he can do about it, though, or about being late to school for the umpteenth time.

"I don't really know if they'll believe it or not," he wheezes, nodding toward the administration offices. "It's like totally apparent there was a fire in my kitchen." *Cough, cough.*

The distinction doesn't matter; Zef will have to stay after school and serve detention, which is a waste of time.

"I mean, it's completely idiotic. You sit alone at a table, doing nothing." *Cough.* "It's ridiculous."

At least he has his six shot, half-decaf, no water, iced venti Americano, hiding in his blue plastic Nalgene water bottle.

"I keep it here," he says, lowering his voice and looking conspiratorially up and down the hallway as he reaches into the inside pocket of his jacket.

"Well, not when there's a hat in here," he says, pulling a large gray wool hat out of his pocket that had been preventing him from hiding his bottle.

Coffee has a downside. One of his teachers got mad at Zef a few days ago for leaving a condensation ring on the teacher's desk. While Zef is describing how this makes the teacher a complete douche, a friend walks past and mumbles something.

"Shut *up,* Josh Lipinski!"

Things in Zef's social life are going well. The mixing board continues to entertain. So does the girlfriend. And, he got a haircut. Preppy and short, though still longish in front.

"What up, Sumner, you like my haircut, man?" Sumner does. But Zef's friend in the wheelchair does not.

"What *up?*" he calls as she rolls past. "Like my hair?"

She says he looks like "a faggot." The slur sounds oddly affectionate. He laughs. She wheels away down the hall.

Two girls approach.

"Zef. I love your hair! Let me touch it," says one girl.

"You look a little cleaner. It's *hot,*" says the other.

More friends sidle up to Zef.

"Zef, did you cut your hair?"

"Yeah, you like it?"

"I hate it."

"Fuck *you!*"

"Dude. What happened to your hair?"

Despite the new haircut and its benefits, schoolwork is not going so well. Zef is now failing, or close to failing, most of his classes. Sometimes he wishes he could just leave Payton and set up that recording studio in his house. That would be cool. *Cough.*

"Fucking toaster!"

Daniel Patton was selling shoes when he got the call. He had a friend log in to his account, then call him at work with the news. Standing by himself at the sales counter at Nordstrom, he was told he didn't get into Harvard. He was deferred. Daniel didn't come to school the following day. In the next week he does not say that the deferral bothers him, even when other students, friends of his like Emily Harris, have gotten in early to places like Yale, their futures seemingly brightened.

Daniel knows he needs to raise his scores. Out of a possible 36 on the ACT he got a 27. He thinks he needs to get at least a 30 to impress Harvard. He's retaking the test. He must also improve his grades.

Even with being president of his senior class, and a leader in the high school, and youth mayor of the city, and knowing a trustee, and being a stylish dresser, and having an inspirational story, it's not easy getting into Harvard. Daniel will have to wait.

Anthony is sitting against the back wall of the cafeteria with The Girl and three of The Girl's friends, same position as always. When The Girl clears her tray, Anthony informs the other three girls, as soon as The Girl is out of range, that *she's* the reason he smokes pot.

"*Hell.* I gotta go smoke *now!*" he shouts, watching The Girl's backside as it slides through the cafeteria door and out of sight.

The other girls howl. Anthony continues. How come The Girl will not go out with him? How can he concentrate on anything else when he feels what he feels? How can he not smoke? Everything is *her* fault. The Girl's friends are having none of it.

"*Puh-leeze!* Cupid-ass earplugs! You need to take them *out.* It's time to let *go!*" shouts one of the girls as the other two jab their fingers at him, screaming like seagulls around some helpless crab. Anthony protests, but not too hard.

"I ain't got *nothin'* to say."

"You better calm that *down.*"

"Blame *me* for being a good person."

This last because Anthony gave The Girl some flowers and chocolates. Despite his giving nature, The Girl has been going out with "some Mexican dude." Anthony says he's going to kill The Dude.

The loudest of the three girls shouts: "Let it go! Let it go!"

Then she starts a five-minute sermon entitled "Why Anthony Better Stop Obsessing about The Girl."

The other two girls egg her on: "Preach on it! *Preach* on it!"

The sermon reaches its crescendo, the girl flapping one hand in front of her face she's getting so heated. Anthony retreats even farther into his green turtle shell, and just when it appears he can not disappear any farther, the girl lowers her voice and leans toward him and says, not unkindly, "Am I right? Am I *right?* You stupid in love."

Anthony nods and says in a barely audible whisper, *"My opinions on the situation are blinded."*

Aisha shuffles through the school's front door, her jacket pulled tight around her like a sleeping bag. She drives to school except when it snows (her parents don't let her drive in the snow). This morning the streets were clear, but she had to park blocks away from school, and then she forgot her mittens. Even though she was holding a hot mug of Pakistani tea, her hands nearly froze.

Aisha walks past the Christmas tree that has just been erected in the atrium (plastic branches stuck in a metal pole with an orange and blue number 34 Walter Payton football patch on top), and heads to her locker. She doesn't put her coat inside.

The cold weather has been giving Aisha a headache. It's a cold she's never experienced before. It's making her eyes water. She keeps a scarf around her neck all the time. Her hands are always chilled.

Later that morning Aisha is still trying to warm her hands. She's running around the library, though not by choice. She's making copies because one of the colleges she's applying to lost her application. Her process has been complex, especially getting her school in Cairo to send her transcript to colleges in the States. Ten minutes later Aisha flops into a seat by the window, throws her feet up, and starts grumbling.

"It's the *waiting* that's annoying. I just want to get in *somewhere.* Then I'll be happy."

She starts fanning her flushed face with the ends of her long *khandi* scarf.

Aisha's Pakistani grandfather is visiting. He doesn't like Chicago. Too crowded, he says. He misses the peace and quiet of Karachi. It's also too cold in Chicago. When he walks around the Shaikhs' neighborhood he bundles in a long coat, a woolly hat, and dark sunglasses to block the wind.

"He looks like a gangster!" Aisha says, covering her laugh with her scarf.

After his walk, Aisha's grandfather surfs the Web on the computer that Aisha set up for him. He'll fly back to Pakistan before the holidays.

As a Muslim, Aisha finds Christmas odd. All the trees, the Santa hats, the candy canes. For her, the most significant thing about Christmas is that chocolate goes on sale. Her Columbian grandmother is Christian, however, and the family is driving down to Florida to surprise her (the grandmother lives next to the house in Palm Coast that the family has kept during their travels). The drive will be long. Six Shaikhs, one Oldsmobile. Aisha's not looking forward to it, though she is looking forward to the warm weather.

After school outside the front door, students wobble from side to side, hands shoved deep in the pockets of their puffy black jackets, shoulders knocking. They look like penguins huddling against a storm. Once the white-haired polar bear of a police officer chases them off, they waddle to the bus or to cars or to the "L," where an advertisement for Aruba has just gone up over the tracks, a splash of pink against the steel gray of winter.

That night it snows, the first snow of the year. A blanket of white covers Payton. In the morning, maintenance workers push blowers and spray salt and mop the puddles of slush that students bring inside with their squeaking boots.

Boots present a fashion challenge to girls. Wear boots over jeans, or tuck them under? Put boots in lockers and change into flats? Sacrifice warmth for style, style for warmth?

Of course, fashion does not matter as much if you are good-looking, and Anais Blake is good-looking enough to wear ugly boots. Anais is sitting in the second-floor atrium, looking out the window and eating a banana. Her boots are large and brown and embroidered with flowers, which make her feet look like pickup trucks with frilly detailing. But if the goal is to warm and protect her feet, they work.

After Anais hurt her ankle, she went to one physical therapist and then another. Neither knew what was wrong. Finally, a third therapist identified the injury: Her leaping had cramped her calf and pulled a nerve and thrown the rotation of her hips out of whack. The therapist re-rotated her hips, and Anais took

loads of painkillers and the pain subsided, though not in time for her Indiana audition. Her mother called and told them Anais was sick (it is never good for a dancer to admit being injury-prone, and Anais says she is not). She was able to postpone her audition until the winter.

Deep down, Anais is relieved that she didn't have to perform. She can't shake the feeling that hurting her ankle started in some way in her head. A few years ago, Anais competed in Irish dance competitions. She did well. Then she started falling. Inexplicable falls where she, the ablest dancer on the floor, just tipped over. She went to a sports psychologist to try to figure out why. The psychologist helped her see how overthinking can be dangerous in dance. Dancing is mental, but it can become too mental. Knowing that, however, and doing something about it, can be different things.

Once the swelling in her ankle subsided, Anais was able to dance. Over the weekend she performed *The Nutcracker* with her dance troupe, the Civic Ballet of Chicago. Anais was a marzipan and wore an elaborate orange tutu. She danced in all five performances.

When she came to school Monday she was worn down, a physical and emotional wreck. She went home early.

Anais lives with her family in a yellow clapboard house with white trim on a quiet street on the North Side. The nearest cross street is Grace Street. Anais has a canopy bed in her room, and that's where she spent Tuesday. She slept the whole day. On her bedroom wall is a poster of a leaping Cuban dancer, another of Baryshnikov. There's also a photograph of Anais dancing with a member of the Joffrey Ballet named Calvin Kitten. Anais is looking at Calvin and beaming. It's one of her favorite photos.

That night Anais could not sleep, so she read her sister's *Cosmo Girl* and *Teen Vogue*. Then she did sit-ups. Even on a day when she does not dance, it's hard for her not to work out. Hard not to do *something*. Over break, Anais is flying to Miami to dance with the Cuban Classical Ballet.

A tackle football game is stirring up the snow-covered field next to the high school. Eight boys in boots and puffy jackets.

Insulting each other, squinting in the snow's glare, throwing a snow-caked ball. No tackles are made. When someone reaches the end zone he spikes the ball in front of the person he ran past.

"Fourteen to seven, *nigga!*"

Every sentence is preceded or followed by "nigga," the epithet tossed around more casually and efficiently than the ball (with the exception of the one white player, who doesn't say anything). The game deteriorates.

"This is *horrible*. We goin' *home!*" It is. They don't Finally a boy is tackled and the other boys pile on top.

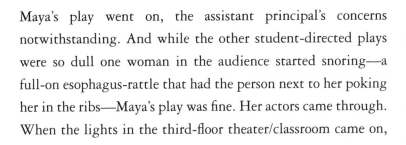

Maya's play went on, the assistant principal's concerns notwithstanding. And while the other student-directed plays were so dull one woman in the audience started snoring—a full-on esophagus-rattle that had the person next to her poking her in the ribs—Maya's play was fine. Her actors came through. When the lights in the third-floor theater/classroom came on,

Maya skipped up to the stage with the other directors and bowed, a big smile on her face.

She's had other reasons for smiling.

Every day, Maya walks home after school. It's one of her favorite parts of the day. After leaving Payton she heads downtown, slowing to look in boutiques or coffee shops or the window display of Barney's New York, and if she's had a bad day, it peels away and by the time she takes the elevator to her apartment on the twenty-sixth floor, she is calm.

When she walked home last Friday, she wasn't calm. She began checking her e-mail every half hour. At eight o'clock the one she'd been waiting for popped up. As she read the line welcoming her to the Stanford class of 2010 she was almost sick. She had to read it again. Then she started jumping around her room. Of the twenty students in the Payton senior class who applied early to Stanford, Maya was the only one accepted.

Maya is also happy because it's the holidays. Christmas is big in the Boudreau family. Maya has been knitting scarves for her sisters, one blue and one purple. She's looking forward to all the festivities. She's also looking forward to hanging out with Anais, and with Ben&Andy. Right now, she's on air, as if nothing in the world could break this bubble, as if this bubble could only expand.

It's the day before break. At the west end of the atrium, the special ed students have wrapped blindfolds over their eyes and are whacking a snowman piñata with a stick. All except the blind. The blind students just grab the stick and start swinging. That they don't need blindfolds dawns on the other students standing nearby and they nudge each other. They also cheer with each swing, and when one blind student crushes the piñata, scattering candy everywhere, the crowd roars.

With the last bell, students pour into the hallways, where they eat cupcakes and unwrap presents and leave wrapping paper on the floor. The cool kids wear Santa hats. Then everyone surges through the front door and into the cold. Snowballs fly overhead. A teacher shouts, "You have permission to be gone for two weeks. *Don't come back!*"

Payton is deserted over the holidays, almost. At the front desk a security guard reads a novel. In the hallways two teachers talk in normal non-whispering voices. In the library, chairs remain tucked under the carrels. In the classrooms, chairs are stacked while floors are cleaned. Mops lean against lockers.

Outside, through the atrium windows, steam can be seen billowing out of the tops of buildings downtown, making Chicago look like a forest dotted with campfires. Everything is soft, cold, distant. The high school is hushed, as if the building itself were taking a deep breath.

JANUARY

Diana comes back from break looking different. It's hard to tell how initially. She's wearing the same plain jeans, a plain T-shirt. But, there it is. In her right nostril. A stud.

Diana's best friend Sandra had wanted a nose stud forever. Diana had also been tempted. Some friends said a nose stud wouldn't look good on Diana because she didn't have the right nose. Too fat. Diana didn't listen, much. Last year, Sandra and Suki got matching angel-wing tattoos on their hips but Diana backed out at the last minute. Not this time.

First they had to find the right person to do it, especially since Sandra was underage.

"A neighbor who is single and thirty, but acts eighteen, she knows a guy. And he knows a guy who works in a shop. This guy couldn't do it, but a friend of his could."

The friend of the guy who knows the neighbor made them fill out lots of paperwork, which took a long time. The piercing didn't. When the needle slid into Diana's nose it felt like a pinch.

Diana avoided her parents for a couple of days and didn't go out of her way to tell them. Her seven-year-old brother did. The family was watching television after Christmas when he turned on the lights and pointed at Diana's nose and said, "See? I told you so!" Diana's mother didn't say anything. Her father was working that night and didn't see the stud until the weekend, and when he did he didn't say anything either. Diana says, "They didn't like it, but they figure it's not as bad as it can be."

There are more pressing concerns for the Martinez family. Diana's brother is still in jail. The police informant didn't show up for the first few court dates, so her brother had to spend Christmas and New Year's locked up in Cook County. The family went to visit over the weekend. Everyone was on edge. They found when they arrived that the brother had been in "the hole." Diana didn't know what "the hole" meant. When the correctional officers told her, they were rude about

it, "treating someone bad just because they're related to someone they think is bad." This made Diana furious. "What does that *mean?!*" she yelled at the officers. One of her sisters told her to shut up, raising her hand in a feint as if she were about to slap her, and Diana, in a preemptive strike, punched her sister in the face.

Diana walked out of jail, her sisters clamoring behind her.

"Get in the car!" they yelled, but Diana kept walking down the avenue, heading toward home. As she turned on 26th Street, the barbed-wire-topped wall of the jail gave way to smoke-churning factories, sheet-metal auto-repair shops, and browned-out lots covered in frozen weeds. Diana walked past it all, her sisters trailing her in the car, driving the same speed she was walking.

At first, Diana stayed angry. *They think I'm not going to walk. I* am *going to walk.* As she kept going, she thought about next year, where she was going to be. She thought about her applications, the colleges where she was applying, the financial aid that would get her there. She thought about this walk and how it was giving her some exercise.

Then Diana didn't think. Her sisters were driving ten feet to her left, honking and yelling through the car windows, but

Diana tuned them out and just kept plowing ahead. In some curious way, it was nice to be by herself, at least until her parents drove up in their car and made her get in.

As Diana talks about her walk home, a phys ed class jogs past in the hallway. Diana watches them turn the corner.

She is not supposed to swim for six weeks because of the stud in her nose, something about the threat of infection. She's thinking of ignoring that and getting back in the water.

"For the most part," she says, finger on the side of her nose, "I think it's healed."

Students come back from break with a little something more, a little something less. One student has new vertiginous five-inch heels. As she wobbles down the stairs, unsteady as a baby taking its first steps, it is debatable whether she can pull this off. Next period she's wearing flats.

Ms. Murphy comes back from the holidays different too. Instead of the gray sweaters she usually wears, she's wearing a loose green sweater over a small belly. She's pregnant.

There's also something missing at Payton. Something in the atrium. There, on the bench under the stairs. A space. Someone who is not here. A few days pass, a few days more. Zef Calaveras did not come back to Payton this semester.

A tray clatters to the floor in the cafeteria, sending a spray of mashed potatoes everywhere. The heavy girl from whose hands the tray fell stares at it—*the nerve!*—then keeps walking. A security guard sees her and barks, "No you don't!" As he points at a broom leaning against the wall, the girl stares at him, at the broom, at him. His arm does not lower an inch. She takes the broom—the students at the tables nearby have stopped chewing—and swipes at the linoleum. After she leaves, the security guard throws a towel over the remaining mess. He shakes his head. "*Oooeee!* You can really hurt yourself on mashed potatoes!"

Not noticing any of this is Anthony Johnson Jr., back against the cafeteria's rear wall, surrounded by girls. Anthony is wearing baby-blue sweatpants, a baby-blue sweatshirt, and blindingly white sneakers with baby-blue trim. On top of everything, the green turtle shell.

He's trying to explain some situation to his cousin, who is sitting across from Anthony and leveling a stare at him so blistering it could warm the french fry dangling from his finger-tips, which he seems to be holding up between the two of them in an attempt to ward her off.

Something happened with his cousin's wallet. She left it on the floor of the cafeteria yesterday. Anthony picked it up. He meant to bring it to her but then he ran into The Girl. The Girl wanted to go to her home on the South Side. Anthony went with her, and his cousin's wallet went with him. He called his cousin from the train and told her he'd come back to school and bring her wallet after he was done with The Girl, but when the cousin called back to find out how long that would be Anthony didn't answer the phone.

He didn't answer because he was listening to The Girl on *her* cell phone—she'd gotten one since the missed meeting at the McDonald's in the fall—talking with The Dude. The Dude, from what Anthony could overhear, was pressuring The Girl to have sex with him. She was saying no. Anthony tried to be supportive, telling The Girl in between the times she hung up on The Dude that she should "straighten out her situation." He was being a good friend, he says.

Anthony's cousin rolls her eyes.

"Press Pause!" she shouts, her forefinger jabbing an imaginary button an inch from Anthony's nose (the protective french fry has since disappeared into his mouth). Then she tells the other girls at the table what *really* happened: Anthony took her money. That is *all*.

The cousin gets up and stalks off with a backhand wave. Anthony keeps explaining his side of the story to anyone who will listen. There were extenuating circumstances. He and The Girl were in the middle of an important conversation. They were working things out. And, she was slapping him.

It all started because of what happened back in the fall, that time they ditched school and went to his house. Around that time Anthony had been talking with some guys in the neighborhood who knew some other guys who set him up with some dope to sell. But he couldn't move anything, so he enlisted his younger brother. Business picked up.

The Girl didn't like him dealing. When they arrived at his house that day, he told her he needed to bag some of the pot in the room he shares with his brother, the room with the huge poster of the scantily-clad aerobicizing black women from the late '80s. The Girl went to his bedroom. After he was done bagging, he walked in and there she was lying on his bed. A girl on a bed. What was he supposed to do?

"If we don't do anything for a while," he says with a shrug, "we end up doing something."

Afterward The Girl was crying but would not tell Anthony why. Her silence made him angry so he threw a sneaker at the wall, which is what his father heard from downstairs. His father came up and searched the place but didn't find anything (The Girl was in the closet behind some coats), though this was small relief as, in the most significant development from that afternoon, The Girl got pregnant.

Or so The Girl says. That's the reason she gives for slapping Anthony on the train. And though she tells Anthony he won't have to do anything with her and the baby, that she's relieving him of all responsibility, Anthony feels stuck. He feels he should do the right thing, whatever that is. The crazy part of all this is that Anthony is not even The Girl's boyfriend anymore. She's going out with The Dude.

"I don't know what's going on!" Anthony calls out, eyes bugging even larger than normal. "You want to know. But do you *really* want to know?"

He slaps the table.

"Until she get a fat stomach or another dude, it's the wait-and-find-out-method."

Adding to his problems, as he and The Girl were riding the train back to Payton, someone robbed him. Or, someone robbed Anthony's cousin, taking the cash out of her wallet in Anthony's backpack. Now Anthony has to pay his cousin ten dollars. His reward, he says, for being a good guy.

Anthony stops telling his side of the story. The girls at the table are long gone, leaving him staring into space. There's little left to say.

"That was my yesterday."

AP biology has a higher percentage of gawky students than the rest of high school. It's scientifically provable. More skinny kids, more squat kids, more pimples, more unintended mustaches, more striped sweaters (more sweaters, period). One lab group is particularly ungainly: a girl with too-tight jeans and limp hair, a boy whose unshowered hair looks as if it doesn't want to be in the room but can't decide which door to exit through, a lanky boy in dress shoes one size too big.

The lab group is running an experiment on DNA sequencing. As they squirt blue marking dye on micropipettes and slide them into trays, they make small talk:

"You using the *electrophysylater?*"

"After we *electro paracify.*"

Then the trays are placed into a humming centrifuge, where the particles are separated into their various elements, in much the same way that the centrifuge of high school has separated these students into AP biology.

After biology class is over, Daniel Patton walks through the halls, dress shoes squeaking. He's holding to his ear the Palm Treo 650 smartphone he got for Christmas. After checking his messages (none), he puts the Treo back into his new leather shoulder bag. With the new bag and the new phone, Daniel looks less like a young politician, and more like a young Wall Street banker.

Daniel doesn't know it, but the Harvard admissions office has been calling his guidance counselor. They're inquiring about Daniel's scores and his grades, wondering if they have improved. Daniel took his ACT again and his score went up slightly. His grades are the same. The word is that if there is any way for Harvard to admit him, they will.

Phys ed has moved indoors to the gym. They're playing badminton. Not badminton, really, but a game best described as Hit the Ceiling with the Birdie. The gym is alive with parabolas, everyone swinging their rackets and singing along to the R. Kelly song blasting from a boom box. If the point of phys ed is to exercise, though, then Hit the Ceiling with the Birdie serves its purpose.

After ten minutes, even this exertion proves too much. Some girls get the idea of playing badminton prone. The developing philosophy for phys ed seems to be *Why do something standing up when you can do it lying down?*

Emily has new green contacts. Why? Why not. Given Emily's coloring, the green is somewhat incongruous. They relax her appearance, though, making it less severe as she strides from class to class. Not that she's gone soft or anything.

Emily's soccer team lost in the championship game of their practice indoor season. The game went into overtime and Emily didn't know that overtime was sudden death and she passed to a teammate who lost the ball and then the other team scored.

Emily blames herself. She blames herself for passing. She says she could have dribbled around the other team and shot and scored, no problem. That's what she says.

Later she wonders, why *didn't* she take that shot? In an unguarded moment, Emily says she hates shooting.

"I don't want to miss. I'd be embarrassed," she admits. She hasn't figured out why this is so, but deep down inside her is this hang-up.

Her fear of shooting started with her club team, the Windy City Pride. When Emily began playing with the Pride she saw that her skill lay in passing. Her coach saw this too, and encouraged it. She became the player who led the team to the goal, not the one who scored it.

Goal scorers are free spirits, impulsive and ballsy. Emily is not that. She's routinely the best player on the field, with technical skill far above anyone else's. But she's a perfectionist. If she's not going to do something well, she's not going to do it, and over time that has prevented her from taking chances. It's the flaw in her game.

Emily says she wants to improve her shot. She knows she needs to work on it for her team to do well in the upcoming season. But how do you improve your shot if it's not in your foot, but in your head?

—

Final exams. The *pock-pock-pock* of the Ping-Pong tables has been replaced by the scratch of pencils and the clicking of laptops. Teachers stand at the front of classrooms, arms folded, legs crossed, staring out, thinking about, *what?*

The silence magnifies the sounds that do occur: the footsteps of a student walking to the water fountain, the rumble of the "L," the smack of a blue booklet dropped on its way to the front of class.

Once students finish, there's a lot of free time. Especially for seniors. In the library, Maya is sitting at a table with Ben&Andy. Ben&Andy are making noise and chewing gum and entertaining Maya with stories until the librarian waddles over and tells them to *shhh.*

They keep telling stories. The first is about how Ben almost got busted by a cop for climbing a chain-link fence into a deserted lot. The second is about a party that Andy went to where a house got destroyed, books ripped in half and laundry detergent poured everywhere. Ben begins a third story as he opens a bag of carrots. The story's most engaging aspect, given that Ben talks with his mouth open, is whether or not a carrot will jump out of his mouth and onto the table.

None do. Maya looks at Ben, her right eyebrow raised, her tongue turning her cheek into a tent. The talk turns to everyone's plans for their last semester here at Payton.

"Do as much as we can," says Andy. "But, no schoolwork."

"Yeah, make a mockery of our school," says Ben. "My dream is to suspend two bungee cords in the atrium and have people up there tumbling."

"I'd let loose chickens," says Andy. "Numbered chickens. All over the school. But the chickens would be numbered one, three, four, so that, yeah, when they got rounded up, everyone would be going around trying to find number two. Get it?"

Everyone does.

"See, if I were to let chickens loose," says Ben, "I'd just let them loose."

Shhh. The librarian waddles over again. The talk turns to a whisper, and to dating. Classmates who make out in the hallway, seniors who hook up with underclassmen, girls who have "associated" with every one of their friends. Then, after some hemming and hawing, it's revealed that one-half of Ben&Andy is going out with Maya.

The bell rings. Time for class.

———

Two girls lean against the lockers and argue. They came here to the far end of a hallway so they could not be overheard. However, the acoustics of the hallway are such that everything that the brunette girl says is amplified, and everything that the blond girl says comes out as an indecipherable *"Rar rar rar."* The argument sounds one-sided, and goes like this:

"You yell at *me,* Carey!"

"Rar rar."

"You disrespect me."

"Rar."

"What am I supposed to do?"

"Rar rar rar rar."

"You text message me and it was like *so* rude."

"Rar."

"Whatever. Ha ha ha."

"Rar rar rar rar rar rar rar rar rar rar rar rar rar rar rar rar rar rar rar rar rar."

"I don't know what you want me to say."

"Rar rar."

"Thanks!"

"Rar rar rar!"

"I'm hurt about you too!"

"*Rar rar.*"

"Well, you text message me and tell me that, Carey! You did that for *no* reason."

"*Rar rar rar rar.*"

"You didn't give me a chance."

"*Rar.*"

"My best friend!"

"*Rar rar rar?*"

"Well. *I'm* pissed."

"Rar *rar rar.*"

"You know what? You're the one person who—"

"*Rar rar rar rar rar.*"

"The only thing? The *only* thing?!"

"*Rar!*"

"You're talking about *me!*"

"*Rar* rar!*"

"Why are we still talking about *that*? We're done with that. We're *done!*"

"*Rar!*"

"I'm saying like, whatever, we're—"

"*Rar!*"

"Okay, you know what? That night, when we were out, was *so* disrespectful. It's so rude to get up on someone and—"

"*Rar rar!*"

"That's *not* why I'm mad!"

"*Rar rar rar rar rar rar rar rar rar rar rar rar rar rar rar rar rar rar rar rar rar rar rar rar rar rar rar.*"

"That's *so* unfair of you to say."

"*Rar rar rar.*"

"That was *a while* ago."

"*Rar rar!*"

"Can *you* please apologize for that?"

"*Rar!*"

"You stand there and attack me and you have no idea why?"

"*Rar rar rar rar?*"

"That's right!"

"*Rar!*"

"How am I supposed to talk with you?!"

"*Rar rar?*"

"You know what? We're *done*. We're done as friends."

The two girls part. One up the hall, one down. Both in tears. Five minutes later, the blond girl is sitting at a table in the cafeteria with other friends. The brunette girl approaches and takes the empty seat next to her. They don't speak to each other, but they sit there together until the next bell rings.

The American and City of Chicago flags at the front door are blowing sideways in the rain, snapping like wet towels. Then the rain becomes sleet, pelting ice BBs. Then the sleet becomes walloping balls of hail-snow. Some seniors step one foot outside for lunch before thinking better of it.

The school hunkers down. Classroom windows steam up. In one cozy room on the third floor, an art class paints still lifes. The students squeeze paint out of tubes and stare at bouquets of plastic flowers. Of the thirty students in the room, eleven are listening to iPods. There's a low-level hum, one that changes depending on where one is in the room. The music shifts from emo to rap to punk, separate weather fronts of music.

Downstairs, Aisha is getting ready for her own art class.

She's in a prickly mood. She's talking about a recent episode of *Oprah*. The show was confronting taboos like premarital sex, and it made Aisha think about high school. Aisha feels there's a liberal conformity at Payton that does not tolerate other points of view. Anyone who questions the accepted line gets a what's-*wrong*-with-you stare. She feels *she's* liberal but the conformity here makes her feel conservative, or at least anti anti-conservative.

"I feel like consensus in this school is . . . " Aisha hesitates, gesturing with her hands as if she's trying to squeeze air into a bag. She believes she's often the only person in class who has a different opinion. This can be intimidating. Just yesterday, her English teacher told their class that media was the single biggest influence on American children today.

"I'm like, *no!* I didn't grow up that way," Aisha snaps. "I'm *definitely* shaped by my family. And everybody else in class was convinced he's right. And I know that he says things to provoke us, but I'm like '*Why* do the kids just go along?' It's frustrating."

Over break, Aisha drove with her family to Florida. After dropping their Pakistani grandfather at O'Hare for his flight back to Karachi, they took the rear seats out of the family van (an Oldsmobile with 200,000 miles on it), laid down some sleeping bags, and headed south.

Aisha drove at night. There was no good radio, and the CD player broke. She drove until Georgia. After her shift Aisha lay in her sleeping bag and read *A Heartbreaking Work of Staggering Genius*. Then she slept. She woke up in the driveway of their house in Palm Coast. Her grandmother was very surprised.

Over the next days, Aisha swam in the ocean and lay on the beach. One night, her elder brother went out with his international friends. Aisha's parents told him to take her, so Aisha tagged along and they all ended up playing poker.

"The best part is that I won!" She giggles. "I took all of their money! I got four of a kind like four times!"

Her brother's friends knew Aisha was a novice. They kept raising the pot, trying to strong-arm her into folding. But, she says, "I don't know *how* to fold. And I wanted to see how it would turn out."

The last hand came down to two players: a boy from Daytona Beach Community College, and Aisha. The community college kid was complaining, "I can't believe it's me and a *high schooler*. A girl!" But the cards kept coming, Aisha kept holding, and at the end of the hand, there they were: four sevens. She took the forty-dollar pot and treated everyone to ice cream. She got banana, her favorite.

As Aisha talks, her earlier irritation melts. Maybe it's talking about someplace warm, maybe it's talking about her family. Their idiosyncrasies are comforting, even as they exasperate her. Fitting in with her family is never a question, a foundation that allows her to be daring in other parts of her life.

Aisha starts packing her books for class. There, inside her backpack, is a blue jersey. Aisha is trying out for the soccer team.

The temperature drops further, if that's possible. A cold that is piercing and cruel. A cold that forces those outside to come in quick, gloves on cheeks. In front of the high school, an adult parks her car, balancing a steaming cup of coffee on its roof, then knocks it over. As the coffee spills down the windshield, it is already freezing.

Anais Blake pulls the sleeves of her tight maroon shirt over her wrists and stares out the atrium window. An icy scree covers the sidewalks, frosts the cars, cakes the tree branches. Anais looks south. She wishes she were in Miami.

Over break, Anais performed there with the Cuban Classical Ballet. A friend who dances with the group invited Anais, as they needed extra dancers for their holiday performance. Anais danced in the back, mesmerized by the Cuban dancers in front of her. The Cubans were the most incredible movers she had ever seen. Just to be part of their performance was thrilling.

As Anais describes the evening—the Cubans leaping, the crowd standing and cheering—her face glows. She almost chokes up. Then, in the slightest of shifts, her teary eyes turn despairing.

Being in high school is suffocating her. Anais missed a week of school when she was in Miami. She's been struggling to catch up with her schoolwork, which holds less and less relevance to her. Sometimes she wonders why she's in high school at all.

An underclassman shuffles past on his way to the bathroom, his hall pass slapping into his heels.

"If you want to dance, *dance*," Anais says, eyes dry now. Making her feel even worse is the fact that a few days ago she hurt her ankle, again. This time, her left. She was leaping *grande allegros* across the studio floor when she felt something wrong, and fell down. She kept dancing, which wasn't smart. But in dance there is such pressure not to be injured (and not to *tell* if injured), which exacerbates injuries further. Anais had just been given a lead in her company's spring performance. When eventually she told her instructor about the sprain he was silent, shaking his head and walking away.

Anais hasn't danced in two days. Her ankle is puffy. And like the last time she was hurt, she has a big audition coming up, this time for Juilliard.

There's a new folding table in the atrium. Taped to its edge is this note:

Angry? Sad? Stressed from school?
Frustrated at home? We want to help.

It's a program run by a psychological institute at Northwestern University. The psychologists sit at the table, staring into space. One has been doing a crossword all morning. The other has a research paper lying in front of him entitled "Rationale for Psychological Skills . . ." which he is not reading. It would seem that one psychological skill would be to recognize that it is not smart to set up a table advertising mental help in a place packed with students who would notice who approached the table and asked for help.

"Welcome to semester two! The last semester of school! How lovely is that?" Ms. Murphy says, seeming particularly peppy today, her curly red hair bounding around like a tetherball in a windstorm. As she circles her classroom, her belly serves as a shelf for her copy of *Crime and Punishment.*

"Can I have a mandatory volunteer?" she jokes. Andy, wearing a yellow *Illinois State of a'Maize'ing Creativity* T-shirt, takes that inopportune moment to stretch, unintentionally volunteering himself. As Andy starts reading, Ben stretches and yawns and scratches himself, presenting his hairy belly to his classmates for their viewing pleasure.

Maya, sitting next to him, does not look, though her right foot is circling so fast it could churn butter. Maya's foot stops churning when she reads aloud, the part where Raskolnikov whacks two old ladies in the head with an ax.

The class starts discussing whether or not Raskolnikov is crazy, and for the next forty-five minutes the comments shoot back and forth. Osama bin Laden's name is dropped into the argument. *Boom.* The discussion screeches to a halt, scurrying away from anything too controversial.

"I don't think we have to come up with a definitive answer to the question right now!" pleads Ms. Murphy, a little less peppy than she was at the beginning of class. "Can I bring us back to the text?"

But before that can happen, the bell rings and class is over, and Maya walks out with her new boyfriend.

Later that day, Maya is sitting outside the recital hall on the second floor. It's her favorite place at Payton. She's talking about her new boyfriend, Ben.

"I never thought of him in that way," she says, taking a sip from a water bottle. Maya and Ben have been good friends since freshman year. He's funny and makes her laugh. He's always been cute.

"This year was different. I could feel *he* felt different. I guess I didn't really want to think about him. Would it change our friendship? When he mentioned it I thought he was kind of kidding. I laughed at first!"

Ben told Maya he liked her when she was at his house over break, just before they were planning to go to a movie. They never went. The relationship has been progressing ever since. They're hanging out after school, on weekends. They're hanging out all the time.

"It's been pretty great!" Maya smiles as she peels the label off her water bottle and starts tearing it into pieces. "We're a lot alike. It's so easy."

Part of Ben's appeal comes from what he's not.

"With a lot of other guys here," Maya explains, nodding at a pack of boys walking past with their pants hanging off their rear ends, "they're into different stuff. Partying, drinking, smoking. All that is so boring to me. They tell the same stories and they don't stop talking. I still like them for the most part. They're good people. But they think it's dorky to talk about a play, or music, or a book."

Ben also seems to genuinely care about Maya. And he doesn't look much like a high school student: He may be the only boy at Payton with a five o'clock shadow.

"I see him differently now. It's really nice," Maya says, turning a color not unlike the pink on the label of her water bottle, which is now in shreds. With that she finishes her water with a gulp.

Despite all the time she now spends with Ben, there are other things that require Maya's attention. She has her audition for NYU in a few days (her acceptance at Stanford has not kept her from exploring other options).

Maya has been rehearsing two monologues for the audition. To do so, she retreats to her room. Her bedroom in the Boudreau apartment has a window looking over Lake Michigan, a view so wide and expansive her room could be a glider above the water. The room is clean, its walls uncluttered except for a movie poster from *The Royal Tenenbaums*. Her desk is clean too, with a neat stack of textbooks, an autographed and framed photo of Owen Wilson. Maya's parents gave her the photo a few years ago, more so because Maya loves Wilson's director from *The Royal Tenenbaums*, Wes Anderson. Maya has always been a little obsessed with Wes. Lying next to Owen is a silver angel charm one of Maya's sister gave her to bring to auditions.

For her NYU audition, Maya chose one monologue from Neil LeBute's *Bench Seat*, another from David Mamet's *Speed the Plow*. Maya starts practicing by sitting on the quilt on her bed and memorizing the lines. Then she takes notes on the characters: how they stand, how they walk, how they see the world. Finally she says her lines out loud, playing with the characters as she goes. It's a solitary process, one she loves. She loves how something imagined in one's room eventually becomes real. It's the most beautiful transformation, how an inner world becomes realized in front of others on a stage.

"And for that amount of time," she says, "you are completely someone else."

FEBRUARY

One of the Cabrini Green towers is getting demolished this week. A wrecking ball, big as a small car, swings back and forth from a crane, slamming into the building, revealing exposed walls and jutting rebars, the gutted insides of apartments, the bent lives and years of those who lived here. Despite the winter cold, workers spray water on the debris to prevent it from igniting. Every few minutes, the wrecking ball connects, and in a plume of dust another part of the construction comes crashing down.

The sounds of demolition can barely be heard through the windows of the Payton library, where Daniel is playing with his Palm Treo 650, a phone that allows Daniel to make calls, text message, send and receive e-mail, surf the Web. Today he's using it to make a call, something he's not supposed to do in the library. He finds a carrel far away from the librarian, poking his head up every minute to make sure the coast is clear. The popping up and down makes him look like a prairie dog.

Someone important has been trying to reach Daniel. Someone from some company about some summer internship. The internship was set up by another someone who Daniel met during the Harvard interview process. Daniel answers the phone. Then he's disconnected.

"Oh, *Lord*," Daniel mutters, which for him comes across as blasphemy. He frantically punches numbers with one hand, scratches his new sideburns with the other. The important someone calls back. Daniel hops to another carrel in search of better reception, pokes his head up, swivels his head, pops down.

"Hello. I dropped the phone," he lies. "Uh-huh, uh-huh."

After a few more polite inanities, Daniel says good-bye.

Daniel hasn't figured out how college will be paid for. He's been filling out forms for scholarships. His financial status is complicated by the fact that his mother, who works for the

Social Security Administration, may retire. His father is a paramedic in the county jail. There's a difference between what his parents think they will pay, and what Daniel knows they need to pay. Where will the extra money come from? Daniel won't be making his shoe money, since he would stop working at Nordstrom if he got the internship. Maybe he'll write letters to mentors and ask for assistance.

"There *has* to be money available," he says, tapping his palm with his Palm. Daniel says that after college he'll go to Wall Street, go into debt, do whatever it takes. He won't give up on his dream of being in politics, and for that he knows he must be connected, and for that he must go to the best college, and for that he must . . .

Before he gets too far ahead of himself, Daniel must finish planning for this weekend's winter ball. Does the president of the senior class have a date?

"I don't. I should ask somebody," Daniel says. But before he can finish the thought he sees the guidance counselor walk past, and jumps into his office.

On the bench under the stairs where Zef Calaveras used to hang out, two boys are sharing the headphones to an iPod. One leans, the other lies flat. Ten minutes later the leaning student leaves. The other stays because he has fallen asleep.

Abandoned on the next bench is a paper bag with a soy banana smoothie inside. There's a note held to the bag by static electricity (accomplished by rubbing the note against a plastic folder):

R.I.P.
—our dear friend—
Abby Mopp
She said she was using the bathroom . . .
but she NEVER returned! ☹
may she rest in peace . . .
the only thing left in memory of her is this smoothie.

There are times when Emily doesn't think about soccer. With the start of the season still a month away, she has been focused on tennis.

Emily has been watching the Australian Open late at night this week. She's a bit obsessed. There's a hierarchy of players Emily follows. At the bottom is Justine Henin-Hardenne (Henin-Hardenne and George W. Bush are her least favorite people on earth). When Henin-Hardenne plays, Emily yells at the television, especially during the game where Henin-Hardenne showed no sportsmanship and just *quit*.

Another player receiving Emily's scorn is Andy Roddick. Emily says he's overrated. And, she says, "He thinks he's cute. He's not cute."

There is no middle to Emily's list.

At the top is Venus Williams. And Roger Federer.

"So good, *and* he's cute. I only like people that are good. I admire that. I like people that dominate. There was this *look* he had. He was so calm. Then, he just took over."

Even when watching her idols, Emily has strong opinions. There's a right way and a wrong way. She has expectations about how other people should act.

She often feels this with her friends. She'll e-mail them about something meaningful she's been thinking about, but all they want to do is instant-message about boys. She thinks about boys too, but not to the same degree. Especially when boys are jerks, and don't deserve attention. Like that boy Emily had a crush on in the fall. He lost his cuteness. She's not interested anymore.

Sometimes Emily just wants to stop thinking about expectations. Let her hair down, break free. Over the weekend Emily is going to see the musical *Wicked*.

The atrium remains *the* stage on which to perform for one's classmates. The winter season has had many compelling plays. *Romeo and Juliet and Melissa. Long Day's Journey Up the Stairs. What Proof?* One hit stands out. A tragedy entitled *The Homecoming King Breaks Hearts As He Must Go to Class,* a performance which needs no explanation.

Diana got a new job. She's a lifeguard and swim instructor at Piotrowski Park, a few blocks from her house. She couldn't be happier.

"It doesn't feel like work!" she exclaims, oblivious to some students wrestling on the floor behind her as she walks through the halls, looking more stylish than usual in a new red Eckō shirt. Her stud is shining in her nostril.

When Diana first got back in the pool, the stud hurt a little. It felt as if her nose was getting pierced all over again. But over time, the pain went away. Now, every afternoon after school, Diana is teaching toddlers to swim. She's in the water six hours a day, working in a Chicago Park Service bathing suit. She's making money blowing bubbles in the water, coaching kids to breathe. When she's not working she's swimming laps.

Sometimes her father comes by in the evening before his shift, to talk and drop off some food. Other nights Diana eats when she gets home. She comes home later than when she was working at the day-care center but feels less worn down. A month ago when she came home, she would nap and eat and worry and go to sleep. Now things are different.

"I love this!" she says, almost bursting.

Diana also had great news. She was accepted by the University of Illinois. She will be the first in her family to attend college. As she talks about the acceptance, her smile is as wide as the hallway.

A maintenance worker shuffles past, jangling his keys.

Diana's older brother is still in jail. But since Diana started her new job at the pool she has been unable to go see him during visiting hours, an arrangement that seems to suit her just fine.

"Do you *know* what day it is?" a pudgy girl sings out, bursting through the library doors. Her question must be rhetorical, because all of Payton is covered in pink and red today. Pink roses, red roses, pink princess crowns, pink frosted cupcakes, pink paper hearts taped to all the lockers, red hearts painted on cheeks, red tape cut into initials and pinned on chests. Even the Payton administrators wear pink today (though more than a few teachers wear green, as in envy).

A midmorning Valentine's Day investigation:

100+ students in the cafeteria
37 girls wearing pink or red
3 boys wearing pink or red
50+ students in the library
19 girls wearing pink or red
1 boy wearing pink or red (though it's a red Wisconsin T-shirt)

The gender difference in appreciation for Valentine's Day is one that, over the course of the morning, some see as an opportunity for exploitation. The skinny boy with the big ears from Mrs. Murphy's English class wanders through the atrium until he sees a pretty underclassman in a tight red top. He stops, pulls a pink paper heart off a nearby locker, approaches the girl

from behind, and slides the paper up under the bracelet on her wrist while throwing his other arm around her neck. He gives her a sweet grin. They hug. Then he keeps walking as the girl watches him go, lips parted, face reddening.

Maya has not been in school for a week. She has mono.

The vice president of the United States shot a man in the face with a shotgun in a hunting incident. It's all over the news. As if in a parallel act of violence, there was the first fight of the year at Payton. It started in the cafeteria. Somebody said something, somebody said something back. Then the first somebody, or maybe it was the second, slapped the other somebody in the face. The slappee didn't back down and the two tumbled into the atrium, a space clearing around them as if a boulder had been thrown in a bathtub. Within seconds the two somebodies were separated by security and dragged in opposite directions to tell their sides of the story, the vacuum they created slowly filling with the competing versions of the event as described by the students who had witnessed it to the students who had not.

Over the weekend, Aisha got a chocolate facial. There was a festival in Garfield Park with free chocolate, including a booth advertising the benefits of chocolate exfoliation. How could Aisha resist? She couldn't. That afternoon she felt ill, though she doesn't think it was because of the facial. Monday she stayed home and that's when she got the e-mail from Claremont.

"I thought I would be more excited," Aisha says of her acceptance, sitting now in her library carrel. "But it was more relief."

After taking the Claremont online tour, however, Aisha got more excited and went downstairs and told her parents.

"My mom was having a cow! My dad was like '*I don't know . . .* ' and I was like '*Stop it!*' So I called my brother in California and he was asleep even though it was the afternoon and I woke him up and he was like '*Yeah!*' because that means he gets to use the car since I'll take it to California. Then he went back to sleep."

Claremont is in the same consortium of colleges as Harvey Mudd. If Aisha goes, she will be close to her brother. Aisha likes the idea of living near family. The Shaikhs are thinking of selling their house in Florida and buying one in southern California, though Aisha doesn't know if she likes the idea of living *that* near to family. Aisha's father has also been thinking of moving to Iraq because, for an engineer, there's a lot of work there now. This doesn't scare Aisha. Her father is Pakistani. She says her sisters would like to move back to the Middle East. At times, she would too.

"I miss the freedom," says Aisha, tugging at the sleeves of the University of Texas Phi Delt Fraternity T-shirt a friend from Egypt gave her.

"I had so much more freedom in Cairo," she explains. "Didn't have a curfew. My parents are paranoid here in Chicago. There are all these restrictions here. They think it's safer over *there*. I was treated like an adult in Cairo. I could go to cafes, restaurants."

Aisha straightens her Texas shirt and says, "I miss the people, the Egyptians."

But Aisha always was aware she didn't quite belong in Egypt either. She was an outsider there as well. She belonged to a segment of Cairo, the European and Western part, and that's the part she misses. A place in between.

Aisha has started taking a class in Arabic at nearby Loyola University, since she worried her Arabic was rusty. It's keeping her busy, along with workouts for the soccer team. Last week the team ran up and down the lake in a snowstorm. The weather was stormy and wild, but they all got behind Emily Harris, the captain, and followed. Aisha doesn't know if she'll make the team, but it felt good to be getting in shape, the snow whipping in her face.

It's the city playoffs in boys' basketball, first seed Taft beating thirty-second seed Payton by seventeen points. The wooden bleachers of the Taft High School gym are packed with boys with GO TAFT written on their chests in blue, bouncing up and down and crushing nachos under their feet. The gym is tight, sweltering. The dim lighting adds to the feeling that the game is taking place in a sauna.

And yet the Grizzlies claw back. With two minutes left they're down by five. Then a steal, a three pointer, both teams rushing up and down the court, trading points. Taft misses a shot and with ten seconds left Payton has the chance, improbably, to win.

A freshman has the ball. He is wheat thin (that morning in Mr. Dyson's physics class he seemed so slender and transparent he could have been mistaken for a beaker), but on the court this afternoon he has led Payton with confident drives and deft shots, and as he slices toward the hoop it seems he is about to put the final touch on this dramatic comeback.

The path to the basket is open, then not. Three Taft defenders slam into the freshman (no referee is going to call a foul on a home team on a game's last play), but he manages to rise through them, hover a foot from the basket, and release the ball. Nothing but rim.

The buzzer clangs. The Taft players jump into the stands and hug their families. The Payton players gather their bags for the bus ride home.

The freshman who missed the shot talks to a local reporter. Then he sits on the bench, still in uniform. The gym empties. The only person on the court is a toddler chasing a shoe. The freshman stands and jogs past the toddler to the basket and jumps into the air and lightly touches the rim, placing the imaginary ball into its rightful place.

Anais Blake did not get into Juilliard. She danced well in her audition, her ankle was fine. Her tights were not. During the group callback, Anais wore black tights, not the pink ones she was supposed to and which other dancers were wearing. Now she's wondering if that could be the reason.

She *knows* it's not the tights, she knows she's being paranoid, but *still*. If it *were* the tights, that would be heartbreaking. It's a week after she found out and Anais is still going over every detail and gesture of her performance, stressing about what must have not measured up.

"You have to accept failure, you have to overcome it. I don't know, part of me . . ." She drifts off.

When Anais dances, she feels she gives her entire self. Not just her body, but her soul. It's a *whole* thing. So when someone criticizes her dancing, she finds it particularly painful, as if the deepest part of her has been judged and found lacking. It is so difficult because it is so personal.

As disappointed as she is with the rejection from Juilliard, they weren't even her first choice. Still, it doesn't feel good to not be asked to dance by *the* premier dance school in the country. Seven other dancers from the Midwest were asked.

One of them, a boy from Minnesota, was one of Anais's best friends from Juilliard's summer camp. They even hooked up. They talked about being together in New York, and now that won't happen.

Anais feels doors shutting all around her, or opening for others. Other dancer friends have been deciding where they're going to be next year. Anais's friend from Miami was offered a position with the Boston Ballet.

"I'm so happy for her," Anais says, not looking happy at all. Then she admits, "I'm jealous of her knowing what she's going to do. She has it all set."

Nothing feels set for Anais. She still has her audition for Indiana coming up, along with an audition for NYU. She has no idea where she'll end up.

Yesterday was especially terrible. Both her feet were throbbing. After dance class, her instructor hinted that if her dancing didn't start improving she wouldn't be a lead in the spring show. All her auditioning and performing has also meant that her friendships at Payton are pretty much nonexistent, especially now that Maya has mono and hasn't been in school. Last weekend, some high school friends called but she didn't go out. Though, when dance friends called with tickets to the Joffrey Ballet, she went.

Her dance friends understand the pressure Anais puts herself under. Like the boy from Minnesota. They relate well, though they haven't talked as much since the summer. Minnesota is far away. She's thinking of asking the boy to prom.

It would be awkward. Anais's little brother and sister are constantly underfoot and that would be embarrassing. The boy from Minnesota would have to stay in the basement.

"Everything's up in the air . . . The whole thing is really tricky. . . . Actually, the situation is a little more complicated," she says, face flushing. "He has a girlfriend."

At one end of the cafeteria, a girl with stringy blond hair and thick black glasses sits at a table studying. Her left hand is covered with handwritten song lyrics and random thoughts:

Don't be surprised when I look in your eyes
and decide this is what I've been missing
shut (the fuck) up!
such a good liar
Now I'm head over heels like the first time I met you
Je ne suis pas fini
give me back my life

At the other end of the cafeteria there is less studying and more shouting.

"The wife went and got *milk!* Left the husband, left the *kids,* left with the *milk man!*"

It's the girl who is always preaching at Anthony.

"He starting to *realize.* He still a *little* hooked. Ain't that right, *'Tone.*"

Anthony nods but he's not really listening. He's playing with the preaching girl's cell phone, punching its buttons. He doesn't have his phone since his parents confiscated it along with his iPod.

"I ain't got *nothin',*" he mumbles. Anthony does have a brand-new White Sox hat, complete with silvery MLB sticker on the brim's underside. Leaving the sticker on, he explains, shows pride of ownership. As he texts and talks, the preaching girl sees she's not getting Anthony's attention and cracks open a history book with a friend.

Last Friday, Anthony went to a party and lost track of time and came home late. That's why his parents took away his iPod. Then his mother searched him and found a blunt in his jacket pocket, so they took away his cell phone. Anthony is failing almost all of his classes. Last month he tried to transfer out of Payton, but no other high school could take him at this late date. He'll have to stay where he is.

His mother also guessed that something happened between him and The Girl. A few days ago, Anthony's younger brother (who recently got kicked out of *his* school for "gang-related activity") was teasing Anthony about how he preferred skinny girls and how The Girl was skinny but "she ain't going to be no more!"

That was a clue.

Saturday morning, The Girl called Anthony and said she was thinking about him. Saturday afternoon she called and said she was going to have an abortion. Saturday night she called and said she wouldn't have it, or wouldn't without telling him. Sunday morning she didn't answer the phone when Anthony called, and when he eventually reached her that afternoon she told Anthony she'd been to the doctor and didn't feel well.

At first, Anthony was angry.

"I had gotten attached to the situation," he explains. He would have helped with the baby. He would have been a great father.

"I could've handled it." He nods. The two girls across from him don't look up from their history textbook, but raise their eyebrows. Anthony responds.

"For real, for real, for *real*."

He felt relief, though. And doubt. The whole time he suspected The Girl was not telling the truth, inventing a pregnancy to keep him jumping. She's the type of girl who would do that. But the result is the same: no more baby, even a hypothetical one.

A boy walks past selling chocolate for some program. Anthony flips a rumpled dollar at the kid, then gives the bar to the preaching/studying girl across from him.

"I got some chocolate! I got some chocolate!" she squeals,

jumping up and down. Anthony jumps up—for someone who spends so much time hunched inside a jacket he moves with surprising speed—and gives her a hug. He gives her something else too.

The girl screams.

Anthony flops back in his seat, a little smile pushing up the fuzz on his upper lip. During the hug he squeezed her rear end.

"I was in fear of my life!" the girl yelps as she unwraps the chocolate bar and takes a bite. Then she fans herself with the wrapper, face flushing, and dives back into her history book, taking periodic breaks from memorizing the dates of Civil War battles to look across at Anthony, who's looking at her looking at him, back and forth, on and on.

"This is most unfortunate!" she cries.

Later that day in physics, Anthony is talking with the same girl when he's supposed to be working on an experiment involving a roller coaster and a marble to calculate potential energy. The students use rulers to make measurements, but Anthony uses his to scratch his back, and to tap the girl's backside. She punches his arm in response. He mouths *ouch* and taps her again, ignoring the small black marble in front of him rolling down its narrow wooden groove.

Overnight, the Payton atrium is plastered with posters for the student treasurer election:

"NOT VOTE FOR FHATTY?
WHY THAT'S JUST WACKY!"
FHATARAH FOR TREASURER.
© 2006 *Paid for by Friends of*
Fhatty.

"For my fourth birthday I asked for
a toy cash register."
Vote Sherman for Treasurer

MARCH

The singer looks like Zef Calaveras but he's not. It's Andy, the more talented half of Ben&Andy. Guitar in lap, he takes a seat on the stage, peers up through his bangs into the spotlights, and clears his throat.

"This song is going to be a bit derivative," he says. The audience shrieks. His words aren't really heard. He starts playing, with lots of wailing and guitar reverb. The audience shrieks *more*. Talent does not have to be understood.

Tonight is talent night and the recital hall is packed, the darkness pricked by a constellation of cell phone screen lights. After Andy, three girls in tight American Apparel–ish shorts and bulky Nike knee pads dance to a medley of recent hits. A girl from the audience struts down the aisle and starts dancing next to the stage. Then another. The aisles fill to the point where there no longer really is an audience or a performer.

Then on go the lights, and as at the homecoming dance, the crowd shouts "Oh-*eight!*" "Oh-*seven!*" "Oh-*six!*" at each other before finding their friends and heading off to parties (though it appears some parties have already started in the bathrooms).

On the field next to the high school, a pack of kids gather in the dark. They're the cool white kids: the boys with the pouty-lipped trucker hats, the girls with bodies that chilly weather can't put a wrap on. Some light cigarettes. One girl jumps on a boy's back and they run across the field yelling, "Oh, the *burn!*"

A tall boy trips a girl and steals her boot, holding it over his head as she jumps in the air, making her grab him around the waist. As she tumbles him to the ground, friends pile on. It's a crisp night, but these kids are hot and they know it. Other kids stand around and watch, looking for an entrance into the act. The most indispensable talent is figuring out how to belong.

Daniel Patton walks into the library, glancing at the sign taped to the library door:

Tired of being lame?
Want to look good & be skilled?
JOIN
THE
Knitkateers!!
– PAYTON'S PREMIER KNITTING ASSOCIATION –
TODAY
Meet after school in the library on Mondays!!
We will teach you to knit.

He settles into a carrel, sighing, "Senioritis is kicking my ass." It must be if Daniel is swearing. He is wearing pressed black pants and a blue button-down Polo shirt. He opens a textbook but doesn't make much pretense of reading.

His mind's not in it. Nor is his mind on last weekend's winter ball, which he organized, or on the girl from another high school who invited him to a Bulls game. Daniel's not interested. His mind's not on girls. His mind's not on shoes, or on money. His mind is on the moment he finds out from Harvard.

"I try not to think about it too much," he says, the flat expression on his face giving every indication that he's thinking about it all the time. On the day he will find out, Daniel has a dentist appointment. Maybe he'll be in the chair, logging on with his Treo, a suction tube hooked into his open mouth. Or he'll find out when he gets back home to his brick house on the South Side.

"I'm going to have my video camera above my computer so I can film my reaction," Daniel jokes, not laughing. He places a piece of gum into his mouth, and starts turning the pages of the textbook. Daniel is sitting mere feet from the guidance counselor's office, but there is nothing the counselor, nor he, nor anyone, can do now.

"I think I may open up the Harvard e-mail right away," he says, nodding, looking as if he made a significant decision. "I don't know."

In a few weeks, he will.

Spring is here. On the sidewalk in front of the high school the snowbanks have thawed, revealing piles of dog shit that had been hiding all winter. Inside the school there's a similar thawing. Long sleeves exchanged for T-shirts that reveal wider swathes of skin. The warming is deeper than skin, though. It's in everyone's brains, affecting students as they bounce from class to class. After school a boy runs through the halls shouting, "School's over! *Weekend!*" even though it is Tuesday. Spring is *here!*

Not quite. In Chicago, spring is a tease. The following day it snows.

On the field next to the high school, the girls' soccer team

is holding one of their first practices. Snowflakes swirl above them. The girls huddle in sweatpants and sweatshirts, hands clenched inside their sleeves. Emily, in a gray sweatshirt with *PRIDE* on the back, leads the team in stretches, then a game

of keep-away. She runs around in her duck-shuffle, encouraging her team with shouts of *"Good job!"*

Inside the library, Aisha looks out at the falling snow. She didn't go out for the soccer team after all. The practices interfered too much with her Arabic class. So after a month of workouts, on the day before tryouts, she decided not to. Maybe she'll paint sets for the school play, or take up yoga.

Aisha is wearing a lilac shirt today whose oriental pattern and soft fabric make it look as if it would be comfortable for *Ardha Hanumanasana.* It's made by Abercrombie & Fitch.

"I used to hate Abercrombie & Fitch," Aisha says with a sigh, "but now I just can't help it!"

Her ensemble is also suffering from an absence of Pumas. She's wearing a clunky pair of Keds. It's her sister's fault.

They had a big fight this morning. It started when her sister asked to borrow Aisha's favorite orange pair of Pumas. Aisha said no. Then her sister asked to borrow one of Aisha's shirts, and before she could say anything, went to her closet and just took it. Meanwhile, Aisha was trying to retrieve some perfume she'd loaned to her sister, and locate her favorite Pumas. She settled on Keds instead.

Thus disorganized, the Shaikhs piled into the car. Aisha's

sister ran back to the house to get her cell phone, but didn't find it. As they sped to school, her sister grabbed Aisha's phone and when Aisha grabbed it back, she saw, hiding under her sister's backpack, her favorite orange Pumas.

Aisha shouted, "This is the last time you wear my shoes!"

They drove on yelling at each other and when her sister got out at Lincoln Park High School, Aisha's Pumas went with her (it was determined that Aisha couldn't make her sister go to school barefoot). But it's a pattern: Aisha lends her sister things, her sister loses things, then gets offended when Aisha won't let her borrow more things.

"All I know is that when I go home today, I'm taking all my shoes back," Aisha says, scowling and kicking her Keds in angry little lurches across the library rug. "She's gonna suffer next year. When I take all my stuff, she'll be all like 'wa wa wah!'"

Aisha has made her decision about college: She's going to Claremont. She's excited. When her father, who had been hesitant initially, saw that she was being given a sizable scholarship, he got excited too. It's good knowing her plans are settled. It allows her to make other plans, like for summer. The Shaikhs are going to Pakistan for a cousin's wedding.

Whenever Aisha is in Pakistan her relatives try to marry

her off. This summer she thinks the effort will be even more intense, especially from her grandfather. Last time, it was non-stop. Mothers came to where the Shaikhs were staying and Aisha had to bring them tea so they could look at her. This never happened to her brother. He wasn't making money, not yet viable. Aisha is fair game. She's past sixteen, and female.

Before any matchmaking can happen, though, Aisha must do some matchmaking of her own: prom.

"I can't *not* go to my senior prom," Aisha says, lacing up her Keds before heading to art class. "Maybe I'll take my sister."

The King of Ping-Pong has been knocked off his throne. He was unbeatable, until today. The usurper is old, in his thirties. He's wearing blue Adidas sweatpants, a red Adidas shirt over a small gut. With each shot, the Adidas man backs up until he's almost standing in the cafeteria doorway, and from that position he sends shots that skitter off the edge of the other side, winner after winner. He's *toying* with The King. He begins to hit shots that whoosh into the heights of the atrium with so much backspin that when they land on the other side of the table, they head back toward the cafeteria, sending

The King scrambling. The game is turning into a show.

A crowd gathers. The Payton baseball team, on their way outside to practice, circles the table: hats pushed back on heads, bats over shoulders, mouths slack. A strand of spittle even forms in one boy's mouth as he stares at the Adidas man. Who *is* this guy?

They don't know that he is Ilija Lupulesku; that "Lupi," as he is known, used to be the U.S. National Men's Singles Champion; that he comes to Payton at the invitation of the Ping-Pong club. But if they did, would that change the expression on their faces?

"We don't have any scoring. That's a problem." Emily scowls, looking out the atrium window at the darkening clouds. She pops a red Skittle into her mouth.

The team has been winning games 1–0. As the center midfielder, Emily's responsibility is to distribute the ball to her forwards. But her forwards are freshmen and inexperienced. One is Emily's younger sister. She's fast and strong, but still learning to score. Emily hasn't scored this season either.

The rest of Emily's game is fine because she's been wearing the same socks. When she plays well, Emily wears the same socks for her next game. When she doesn't play well, she changes them. She also drinks from the same water bottle until she doesn't play well. So far this season, Emily has been drinking from the same water bottle and wearing the same socks.

Payton has a game later today against Lincoln Park, their rivals. *"Northsiders,"* Emily scoffs. There's been some preseason bad blood between the schools. Some Lincoln players said they want to hurt some Payton players, which Emily thinks is foolish.

"We're just better than they are," Emily says, green eyes unblinking, "and they should accept that."

One reason the Grizzlies have been playing well is that Emily has made the freshmen feel at ease. When Emily was a freshman there was one senior girl who never said hello to her in the halls. Emily would never act that way. She's made a point of hanging out with her freshmen after games, being the team's big sister in more ways than one.

"Today, after we beat Lincoln Park, we're getting together."

Emily looks out at the gathering clouds and says, "I just wish we would score more."

With that, she flips the last Skittle into her mouth, a blue one. Emily saves the blue ones for last, for good luck.

———

That afternoon up at Montrose, a turf field next to the lake, the clouds from earlier in the day have darkened and dropped. A cool spring rain blows sideways. Fans lean into umbrellas, and second-stringers peer out from under warm-up hoods. The game is a mess, everyone bunching on the side of the field where the wind has blown the ball, as if the players were food that had slid to one side of a plate.

Weather is an equalizer, but Emily refuses to be equaled. As much as she appears not to run, she may be hustling more than anyone. Side to side, end to end, repositioning herself constantly. Other players let the ball slip away from their feet, but not Emily. At the end of the half she settles the ball, glances up, then drives a pass over the Lincoln defense to her sister, who puts the ball into the back of the net.

As her teammates hug, Emily lingers behind. Hands on hips, white jersey stuck to her front and billowing out from her back like a sail, squinting through the downpour.

Nice try, rain.

Maya walks up the atrium stairs slowly, as if the stairs were a mountain and she were low on oxygen. She was out of school for three weeks.

"It was the worst experience of my life," she moans, taking one more step. "I just lay there. It was so boring. It was the grossest thing ever. My throat was almost completely swollen shut."

She started feeling unwell before her NYU audition. But she kept telling herself, *I cannot get sick. I cannot get sick.* So she did not get sick, and her audition went great. But she knew she was pushing herself too hard, spending too much time with Ben, revving high in a low gear.

"There wasn't any time for me to calm down."

The afternoon after her audition Maya felt a bump on one side of her throat. An hour later she felt a bump on the other side. When she opened her mouth it was coated with whitish gunk. She called her sister, who's a doctor, and the next day went to her own doctor and was told she had mono. That night she crashed.

The first week was dreadful. She'd wake up late, her swollen neck as wide as her head. After popping some ibuprofen she'd watch *Oprah,* then *The View,* then the view out her window of the lake. Sailboats and bicyclists, the world blossoming, with her stuck up on the twenty-sixth floor, as miserable as she had even been. In the afternoon she napped. When she woke she

157

read monologues from Spalding Gray, which were depressing because Gray ended up drowning himself. Then she'd shower and change into new pajamas.

One afternoon, Maya got a letter. It was an invitation to a party for incoming freshmen at NYU's Tisch School of the Arts. This was odd. Maya hadn't been accepted at NYU. After checking online, it appeared she had been. It was exciting, in a backward sort of way. Being accepted was a huge honor since, as Maya knows, Tisch is one of the best acting schools in the country. Maya was thrilled, though it was hard to smile with a

throat coated in pus. After three weeks of lying around in her pajamas, she came back to school.

"I could go to sleep right now," Maya whispers, slumping on the bench outside the recital hall. She still feels sluggish. When she was in the depths of mono, Ben brought her a smoothie (one with echinacea that burned her throat), but now that she's back he thinks that because she looks fine she is fine, which she is not. This has caused tension between the two of them. He expects more, but Maya doesn't have it in her to give.

"It's hard," Maya says, voice fading in and out, "to make excuses."

Mr. Dyson, the physics teacher, is in his patient teacher mode. He's rubbing the top of his bald head.

"We're prepared, almost," he says, staring directly into the eyes of each of the students in his Zulu seminar. His own eyes are bloodshot.

These last months, when not learning Zulu, the seminar has been planning a spring break trip to South Africa, an exchange with a high school in Durban. It's taken a huge amount of work. Every week the seminar becomes a room of travel agents (checking tickets online), fund-raisers (writing letters to Oprah and other institutions asking for money), or U.N. diplomats (making presentations in Zulu and PowerPoint).

"Do you all have your malaria meds?" Mr. Dyson asks, voice rising to be heard over the beat of Skwatta Kamp's *"Washum-khukhu"* playing in the background.

"Yebo!" the students shout. *"Yebo!"*

The students fly to South Africa next week. On Mr. Dyson's desk is a stuffed cat. Students walking into the seminar give the cat a tap for luck.

Diana looks strained, her face tight. It's her free period and she's sitting outside the girls' bathroom on the first floor, holding a copy of Chinua Achebe's *Things Fall Apart*. She's rubbing her hands over the book cover and smoothing its edges. She's not smiling. She feels everything in her life crept up on her and smacked her on the back of the head.

"It didn't hit me until now," she says. "Home and stuff."

Her brother pled guilty. Soon he'll be transferred out of Cook County Jail, serve three months at a detention facility, then return home. This is some relief, since he could have received a two-year sentence. The girlfriend of the police informant, on whose word the case depended, never showed up in court. Diana's brother was able to plead to a reduced charge. Another relief was that some other inmates escaped from jail and asked Diana's brother to join them but he said no. Their escape, and capture, have been all over the Chicago papers.

That's the one thing Diana does not blame her brother for. She blames him for everything else. She blames him for not having a job. She blames him for the big tattoos covering his arms, which make him look like a gang member. She blames him for hanging out on the street all day doing nothing.

"What did he expect?"

It's possible he'll be able to come to Diana's graduation. It's possible he won't. The general uncertainty makes life difficult. Like when her brother's boy comes to the Martinez house and everyone has to tell him that Daddy is at school. Though even something difficult has an upside. Diana loves having her nephew around.

"Oh, *ye-eh-es*. It's nice," she says, smiling for the first time today. Her eyes are watering.

Diana has been sick all week. She can't shake her cold, or her irritation. Even the good things in her life have been upsetting her. Her father is taking his U.S. citizenship exam, and she's had to spend a lot of time helping him study. Her younger brother started swimming, but the other day he didn't want to go to the pool and she had to drag him there.

"I explained to him, 'You get used to it.'"

Despite the many demands on Diana, one thing has made life easier. Scholarships have been pouring in: a Hispanic scholarship, a President's Award, a thousand dollars here, a thousand dollars there. The family share of Diana's tuition at the University of Illinois could be as low as twenty-eight dollars. It's gratifying, though sometimes it's hard to appreciate good news if everything else around you seems to be falling apart or dragging you down or holding you back.

"Time flies. It's amazing," laughs Ms. Murphy, her growing belly ample evidence of the accuracy of her words. Class has separated into groups to check the answers to an AP practice quiz. Given that spring break is days away, it's a struggle to stay on subject. Only when Ms. Murphy is standing within earshot do the groups talk about what they are supposed to, giving the discussions a loopy interrupted quality:

"What's pathos?"

"Could you talk a little more quietly, José!"

"WHAT?!"

"It has to do with style."

"Don't mock me."

"How was your party?"

"Cool."

"We made it, but only outside."

"Ooo. It was pathos."

"That's what *she* said."

"She's such a slut. She's had sex with like twelve people."

"Is she our age?"

"They could put me on probation!"

"I digress."

"Moving on!"

"The question is asking the function of a modifying adverb."

"That's *so* awesome."

"It's hard to get around Los Angeles."

"Are you staying in your hotel room?"

"Her friend has a car."

"We should chill!"

"He's a big dork."

"Writer. He has no life."

"It's gotta be hard. You've got to take one event and relate it to the whole world."

"People. Who's sitting in this chair?" (Ms. Murphy, pointing at an empty chair.) "Okay, so the whole time, I thought someone was in the bathroom!"

"How many people got number seven wrong?"

"You picked *D*?"

"Shut up, Drew. *Shut. Up.*"

"We were trying to do a volunteer show at a nursing home and it was like, booked. The place was classy."

"Nursing homes and classy, aren't they, like, synonyms?"

Anais flew to Switzerland for spring break. Maya was supposed to go with her, but mono changed that. The trip was part of a Payton exchange with a Lucerne high school. There were strict rules. One rule was that, on the free day with their host families, the students could not leave Lucerne.

The boy in Anais's host family was named Dragon. Dragon was Czech, and suave. He'd just turned eighteen and had a brand-new Mercedes (which he had named Shannon after the actress Shannon Elizabeth). Dragon wanted to give Shannon a ride.

So he drove Anais to Italy. As they sped through rolling hills, Anais looked at the small houses tucked in the valleys and tried to imagine what it would be like to live there, so far away from anyone. They drove through a tunnel under the Alps and crossed the border.

Everything felt different in Italy. The architecture, the weather. Milan was muggy. Anais and Dragon walked around the Piazza del Duomo. It was Palm Sunday, and congregants with fronds in their arms were exiting the cathedral. Anais went inside. The interior was serene, and smelled of burned palms. A choir was singing. She sat in a pew and listened. She stayed there, listening and letting the feeling of the place wash over her.

Afterward she and Dragon shopped, and had lunch. Then they got back in Shannon and headed north, stopping in small Italian mountain villages on the way. The villages were captivating. Anais could have spent all day in them. But they kept driving and she fell asleep. She awoke in Switzerland, and never told her classmates or the Payton chaperone what she had done. It was a beautiful day.

The trip to Switzerland was the longest Anais had ever gone without dancing. Almost ten days. It was frustrating, but also wonderful to eat anything she wanted, to be free to drive through the mountains and experience something she never had before. Before she flew home, Anais tried to go to the ballet in Geneva but wasn't able to get tickets.

Spring has come to Chicago. Really, no joke. The buds have opened on the trees in front of Payton. Students break out clothes that were hidden in closets for months. Girls put on sandals, their toes released from their winter caves.

Like the first crocus of the year, the first girl shows up at school wearing a tiny T-shirt that shows not only her belly button but also her pelvic bones as they dip into her pants. This proves irresistible to the nearby boys, who, though they feign indifference, buzz around her like bees around a pistil.

Spring *is* here.

Inside the cafeteria, there's another situation with Anthony Johnson Jr. This one does not involve the girl who was pregnant, or the preaching girl whose rear end he squeezed, but a third girl, who is sitting across from him at his table, mouth open.

"That's not how it happened!" she shouts.

"This should be a *good* thing!" he shouts back.

Anthony is not slumping today. He's almost leaping out of his loose brown TEAM VŌKAL hoodie.

"This is how it goes," he explains to all the other girls at the table, smiling wide and chomping loud on his gum. "I'm in physics, doing nothing like I normally am—know what I'm saying?—and I wrote this letter, know what I'm saying. It was a playing-around letter, just a letter. I showed it to some girl and she took the letter and give it to *that* girl." He nods across the table. "And she took it as a *love* letter!"

"*I can't hear! I can't hear!*" mouths the girl in question, making a show of pointing with her purple fingernails to the headphones she has clamped over her ears.

"What I'm saying is . . . What I'm *saying* is!" Anthony smiles wider, hand reaching across the table. The girl stares at her Chinese language textbook and raises her eyebrows. When he sees she's not going to listen, he takes the opportunity to clear up some details about his situation with The Girl.

It turns out that the baby had been The Dude's. It's unclear how The Girl knows this, but that's what she has told Anthony.

"At first I was like, *uhhh,*" Anthony says, making a face as if he'd been told the Earth was flat. So the baby was never even his, after all that drama. Which also means that the whole time The Girl was telling Anthony she was getting pressured by The Dude to have sex, she was already having sex with The Dude. She was playing Anthony all along.

She wasn't playing her parents. When they found out she was pregnant, they kicked her out of the house. She moved near Anthony. Now she's been reaching out to him, calling late at night and telling him to come over, telling him she doesn't have clothes on. Stuff like that.

"I don't care no more. She took it about as far she could. She did everything she possibly could to me," Anthony mumbles, his mood dimmed from a few minutes ago. He throws his hands out as if pushing away a plate of something that tasted bad.

There are other things he wishes he could push away. His classes, which he's still failing. Tutorials, which he's not going to. Then there are things he wishes he could pull close. His cell phone and his iPod, still impounded by his parents because they found more dope on him. A car, which he's been dreaming of since he turned sixteen.

Thinking about the disparity between what he has and what he wants gives him a headache. Anthony starts rubbing his forehead vigorously. No more headache. That was easy. With the headache gone he starts flicking a lighter under the table, and staring across the table at the girl with the headphones, trying to get her to look at him.

When the girl sees him staring she removes one earphone and yells, "You are such a fucking asshole!"

"But it wasn't like that!" he protests, glad to have finally gotten her attention. She looks up at the ceiling, pleading.

"I can't stand his ass. *I can't, stand, his ass!*"

"If nobody had ever—"

"My feelings was hurt," the girl interrupts, pouting.

With that Anthony reaches his arm across the table, almost touching her hand, and says, "What I said to you is that what I said in the letter was the truth."

But what was the truth? What he wrote, or what he's saying now?

Anthony nods.

Another girl walks up and she and the headphone girl start talking behind the textbook, which they have raised to hide what they're saying.

"I have people whispering about me!" Anthony shouts so that the entire end of the cafeteria can hear. But that doesn't matter. What matters is that the girls are talking, and about him, and to Anthony the situation could not be better.

APRIL

Jonathan Safran Foer, the writer, has come to speak to Ms. Murphy's English class. Foer looks like the young male teachers at Payton, the ones who wear jackets and V-neck sweaters to make sure they are never confused for students. He's small. As he sits at the edge of the recital hall stage, his loafers dangle in the air and don't touch the floor.

 But as hard as Foer may be trying not to look his age, the students know that he's their contemporary. They look at him with wide-eyed admiration as he gives them kind advice about writing and life.

Afterward, they line up to have their books signed,

copies clutched to their breasts. As they get closer to him, the fact of Foer is tantalizing. Here he is, *real*. They can almost reach out and put him in their pocket. After getting her book signed, Maya walks out of the recital hall, face glowing.

"He's so crushable!" she chirps, popping a piece of gum into her mouth. Though it is not clear whether she's referring to Foer's size or his cuteness, it's probably the latter. She heads outside the front door and sits on one of the benches in the sun.

Maya's in a lively mood. She looks tan, healthy. Something else is different too. Over break Maya went to Arizona to visit one of her sisters. Her sister's best friend's husband is a hairdresser and her sister has a pool and one day everyone sat around the pool and had their hair cut. Maya got bangs.

"I think it's worth it. It's working pretty good!" She giggles, scrunching up her nose. "I like it better. Freer. Ready for summer. I don't know what that means!"

Maya is freer in other ways. There's no more boyfriend. Just before flying west, the relationship with Ben went limp. It may not have helped that around this time, he cut his shaggy hair into a mullet.

"We weren't compatible. We just didn't get along that well

as a couple. We clashed. He's very stubborn. So am I," Maya says, sucking her cheeks inward. "It was frustrating."

She stops and starts, circling around what exactly went wrong.

"Fine while it lasted, but it was kind of like, it's better this way . . . .

"We're better off as friends . . . .

"I don't know. I don't know . . . .

"I think it may . . . It was *everything*."

Maya stops chewing her gum. She talks about how she and Ben had gotten very serious very quickly. He wanted sex. She wanted to wait, or at least to take things slower. It didn't feel *right*. After she had mono, after she got better, he got impatient and angry all the time. He wasn't very nice about it. As she talks about her decision to break up with Ben, she speaks with some relief. She's looking forward to making new friends in New York or California.

Maya hasn't decided where she's going to college. Last night she talked late into the night with her parents. They support whatever decision she makes (though some of Maya's teachers shake their heads when they hear she hasn't automatically accepted Stanford). She knows she's lucky to have such a choice.

She knows Stanford is prestigious. But at Stanford she would be a student. At NYU she'd be an actor, and she's always wanted to be an actor.

"I don't know," she says, though it's hard to hear her through the clump of hair that she's pulled into her mouth.

Whatever Maya decides, wherever she goes, tuition will be astronomical. Upwards of forty thousand dollars a year—an impossible number. To earn spending money and buy a new computer, Maya recently got a job at Nordstrom. She'll be working in the teen department. As she mentions this, she claps.

"I feel like such a girl!"

After her interview last week she came home and complained to her mother about how tedious the job would be, how much of an act she'd have to put on.

"I'm like, '*Argh*. I don't belong here.'"

Her mother replied, "'Welcome to the real world, Maya.'"

So before Maya heads off to college (wherever that is), she's looking at a spring and summer of selling fashion to teens.

She cries, "My dream come true!"

Mr. Dyson's students from the Zulu seminar are back from South Africa. As they walk through the halls, they look exhausted.

The flight was long, the trip full. Visiting townships, meeting students from Vukuzakhe High School, painting murals. They even met the Zulu King. His name was Goodwill Zwelithini. He was a big rambling guy who wore linen pants. The students were disappointed that the king's clothes weren't cooler. When they met him, they had to take off their shoes and shout stuff like *"You're the great elephant!"*

One morning they saw a real elephant. After waking under a star-pricked sky, they drove to Hluhluwe-Umfolozi Game Reserve. They headed out in the day's first light and a lone bull elephant walked directly across the path in front of them. He smelled rank.

The students had an overnight stay with their Vukuzakhe High host families. Everyone was apprehensive. It was after dark when Mr. Dyson dropped the students off in the winding streets of the impoverished Umlazi Township. But in the morning, all the students gathered back at the high school, filled with stories. They were somehow bigger now through their connection to high school students halfway across the world.

Next fall, the students from Vukuzakhe High are coming to Payton.

On a second-floor hallway in city hall, a janitor pushes a buffer over the marble. It's six o'clock, after work. The janitor is cranking Aerosmith on a boom box; the wailing of "Dream On" nearly drowns out his polishing, and the meeting taking place next door in the city council chambers.

The meeting is for the YMCA youth council. Twenty-two students sprawl in a semicircle of leather chairs around cloth-covered tables, facing the podium and listening to their youth mayor: Daniel Patton, wearing a Penn sweatshirt.

Daniel did not get into Harvard. The rejection came in an e-mail that began with some perfunctory *"I am sorry to inform you . . . "* Initially, Daniel felt pretty bad. He didn't film his reaction. But the bad feeling improved because, on the same day, Daniel was accepted by the University of Pennsylvania. Penn is the best college that Daniel got into, so Daniel will go to Penn. He says he's excited to be going to such a prestigious school, an Ivy League school. He says he's moving on. It's not like there was anything he could do about his rejection from

176

Harvard, so there was no point moping. But, at least initially, not getting into the school of his choice was a slap. His expectations were derailed and had to be reconfigured, and quickly. One of the first things Daniel did when he didn't get into Harvard was go out and buy himself the red and blue Penn sweatshirt.

Complementing the clothing of his future alma mater, Daniel today is wearing brand-new white sneakers, dress socks, and khaki pants. The youth mayor is handing the seat of power to next year's youth mayor.

"Has everyone who wants to be nominated for mayor been nominated?" Daniel drawls into the microphone, gavel held loosely in his right hand.

After nominations are made, a legislative aide to the real mayor addresses the youth council. The aide is old and white.

The students are young and black.

"Have any of you attended a city council meeting?" the aide asks, hands in pockets, rocking on his toes. Nobody raises their hands.

"How boring was it?!" the aide jokes.

He proceeds to bore the students for

forty-five minutes about how boring the city council is.

Daniel swivels in his leather chair, face drawn up in a responsive smile. The students on either side of him have their hands under the table and are texting on their cell phones. After ten minutes of smiling at the mayoral aide, Daniel pulls out his Treo and starts tapping away too. Then the aide stops, and Daniel lopes up to the podium and takes the gavel.

The youth council starts debating a resolution: Wal-Mart, good or bad. A vote is taken and it's decided: Wal-Mart, bad. As youth mayor, Daniel does not get to vote, though he is the one who must count the votes of those who do.

"Watch number twelve!" shout the mothers of the Francis W. Parker School girls' soccer team. The mothers are thin, which combined with their oversized sunglasses, makes them look like hungry bugs. But they are smart bugs. Number 12 is Emily Harris and she *should* be watched.

Emily is dominating today's game. It's a sunny day, and as she shuffles around the manicured grass field on Parker's Lincoln Park campus, her navy blue jersey and orange socks are shining. The ball never leaves the Parker side of the field. And yet, Emily's team can't score. The Parker players are as wide as their mothers are thin, and size matters. In fact, it roots them to the ground like a wall, and whenever Emily passes the ball close to the goal, one of the walls pokes it away with a toe.

In the second half, a perfectly threaded pass from Emily springs her sister on a breakaway, but the last defender takes her down from behind with a hard tackle. She stays on the ground, Emily bending over her, then is carried off the field.

When play resumes, a Parker player slams into the Payton goalkeeper with a reckless charge. Emily barks, *"Stay the fuck away from my goalie!"* She and the girl jog up the field, shoulder to shoulder, jawing at each other.

Impatience seeps into Emily's game. Her sister, who has emerged as the team's scorer, is no longer there to score. During one stoppage Emily bites her nails.

With a minute to go, Emily tries to win the game by herself. She gathers the ball at midfield, fakes left, fakes right, making one pony-tailed defender miss, then another, then a third. With a final deft touch Emily slides the ball around the last defender. She's alone against the goalie. But her shot hits into the goalie's outstretched hands, and over the crossbar. Emily runs the ball as fast as she can to the corner for the free kick, but time runs out, and who was she going to kick it to anyway?

Afterward, Emily seeks out the other team's captain and apologizes for her outburst. Then she slumps in the middle of the field. There are few things worse than tying a bad team. When she describes the game later that week all she says is: "Awful."

Diana wraps a flotation noodle around the waist of a toddler, pulls it tight, and tosses the toddler into the water. Then onto the next: noodle, tie, toss.

The Piotrowski Park pool is inside a ripped canvas dome. The rest of Piotrowski Park is in a similar state of disrepair. Overflowing trash cans, chewed dirt fields, broken swings. None of which seems to faze the many people using the park today: the grown men playing baseball, the women selling flavored ice and *chicharrón con cueritos,* the toddlers splashing around the pool in bright swimsuits of pink and green.

Diana is wearing a blue Chicago Parks Department T-shirt and chewing ice from a plastic cup. As her coworker begins coaching the kids in the water, Diana walks along the pool deck, signaling with her hands for the children to kick.

On the deck behind Diana, her younger brother is sitting on her nephew. It's so loud inside the canvas dome that Diana doesn't hear her nephew's cries, but when she does she hoists him up and balances him on her hip and goes back to coaching the toddlers.

Her phone rings. A ride for the nephew is arranged.

When class is done, Diana will swim. She's been increasing her laps this spring, so much that she's improved her 200-meter time by ten seconds, a considerable amount. She's noticeably leaner, less round than the fall. When she heads to the Universtity of Illinois, she thinks she'll be even faster. But that is months away. Right now Diana has to work, to lift toddlers in and out of the water and tie the flotation noodles tight around their waists so they don't sink.

Truman College, a community college and end-of-the-line high school, is a metal rectangle of a building next to the red line stop in Uptown. The surrounding neighborhood exudes a lack of charm. Across from Truman there's a Popeye's Chicken, a Starbucks, a Chinese restaurant, some currency exchanges. Down the road there's a stone Baptist church with a white neon sign on top that reads CHRIST DIED FOR OUR SINS. Outside Truman's front door, students huddle and smoke. One of them is Zef Calaveras.

After flicking his butt into the gutter, and hunching his neck into his jacket collar to protect against the unseasonably chilly day, he scurries across the street to the Starbucks. He's waiting for a call from a girl. He looks jittery. After getting his six shot, half-decaf, no water, iced venti Americano, he places his cell phone on the table in front of him, takes off his jacket, and leans back. He's not wearing his black pirate T-shirt. He sips his coffee and sighs. "It's like poison. So good!"

Zef starts explaining his decision to leave Payton, fifty blocks to the south. Well, the decision wasn't his.

"Payton suggested I *'drop out,'* because I'm *'failing,'*" he says, holding his fingers up in exaggerated quotation marks. Then, according to Zef, it turns out he wasn't failing. The whole thing was "ridiculous." But he had seen this coming since the beginning of the year.

"I was doing worse and worse. All these people said 'Everything gets better junior year' and whaddaya know, it didn't."

So Zef was encouraged to leave, and transfer to Truman. Truman is a school in the city that takes students who have failed out of other schools, or been kicked out, or are looking for a second chance. The differences between remedial high school and community college are blurred. There are no sports teams, no music, no art, no homework to speak of ("all that chaotic other stuff," as Zef describes it). Just classes that propel one toward graduation. Students are let out at noon.

"And here's the slick part of the deal." Zef snorts, leaning forward and twisting the paper of his straw cover into a string. "I can go straight from high school to college!"

Zef's cell phone rings. He gives the girl directions. He hangs up. Zef will be able to graduate from Truman next winter, then transfer to a community college, where he can study to be a sound technician, which he says is what he wanted to do all along.

Zef likes his Truman classmates. They all share the experience of not making it somewhere else. Zef fits in, in this school for misfits. Best of all, Truman has given Zef more time to do his favorite thing in the world: hang out in music shops.

"I'm a gear *slut*. I go to Guitar Center and I hang around for hours and *hours*."

"That's me in a pipe shop!" says one of Zef's friends who has come along for the coffee. Zef's friend has scraggly hair and bad teeth and is wearing a camouflage jacket, which all makes him look like Silent Bob's not-so-silent brother. After his piped-in comment he falls silent again.

Zef is not silent. In fact, he's amplified, and his six shot Americano is making him more so. His right knee is pumping triple time. If he were at a loom he would already have woven a blanket.

Zef misses his Payton friends. According to Zef, his friends miss him too.

"They say, 'Shit, *goddam*. Class is like so much not fun without you here!'"

Zef doesn't miss his Payton girlfriend because she's not his girlfriend anymore. She stopped talking to him over break. He leans across the table, looks right, looks left, and whispers some rumors that are scandalous and impossible to corroborate.

"She didn't have time for anything else! Yeah, well. It was just, like, so, *achchhwrspppr*." Zef hacks up a load of phlegm.

"I'm *so* stuffed up. I have terrible allergies," he explains, before proceeding to list them. "Trees. Grasses. Pollen. Ragweed. Mold. Dust. Fish. Meat, which is okay because I'm a vegetarian. I'm allergic to wheat. I'm allergic to soy, which tastes awful. I'm allergic to rice."

Zef is also lactose intolerant. "I'm allergic to cheese, though I do eat pizza. If I drink milk I get *mad* runny nose. You should *not* see that."

Something that Zef is less allergic to now is sleep. He says his insomnia has disappeared since coming to Truman. He's going to bed before midnight. He's not sleeping in class. He wonders if the stress of failing at Payton kept him from sleeping. Since he can't fail anymore, he can sleep.

More sleep gives him more energy for music. All evening, he's been cranking out tracks on his computer. He would share the stuff he's been working on, but his iPod is no longer functioning.

"I pressed it and heard *'wrreeeeeee!'* Something inside it is broken."

Just then, Zef's other new friend, a slight and pretty girl with long brown hair, comes up behind him and throws her arms around his chest. He reaches his arms backward around her, and in that moment, his knee stops pumping.

Aisha is not in the library. She's in a third-floor art room, looking over her portfolio, preparing to show everything to her teacher.

She stands on her toes to point out the pieces strewn over the table (her toes inside the pair of burgundy Pumas she got over break, whose purchase completes her collection of every color of Puma), explaining each: a print of a dove, a print of a handgun, a map of Toledo, a map of Paris, a drawing of a sun, a camel. Overlaying the images are bits of fabric, written Sanskrit, pieces of paper ("When I'm mad or something, I go paper shopping!"), everything cut and pasted. Aisha's hands are sticky with ink and glue.

She also took a self-portrait, presently in a trophy case in the atrium, in Cindy Sherman's style. Aisha's photograph shows her sitting at the edge of Lake Michigan swathed in an elaborate sari, with heavy makeup and a gold hoop through her nose (pierced on a trip to Pakistan and never worn at Payton because she considers it too conspicuous). She looks foreign, and not. Though, what does someone who is half-Colombian and half-Pakistani look like? Someone who was born in Ames, Iowa?

"I don't think anybody's sure where I am from. They're kind of confused," she says.

In America, Aisha is Pakistani. In Pakistan, she's American. It means she's always an outsider, just like in high school.

The Shaikhs have finalized plans for their trip to Pakistan. After graduation, Aisha will fly with her brother to England, take a train to the Netherlands, and drive around Europe with friends from Egypt. Then, Karachi.

It's hot and unpleasant in Karachi in the summer, but that's when her cousin's wedding is. Aisha has loads of cousins. She likes some, others she finds too religious and overbearing. She thinks they are backward, coming as they do from villages with their hierarchy of male elders.

Her Pakistani relatives have their own views of Aisha. Because of outbursts she had when she was young, they nick-named her *Sarely*, which means "whiny one." They thought she was small and opinionated. As with any family, the feelings of closeness, and its opposite, can make things complicated. Sometimes more complicated. Aisha mentions that one of her cousins, to avoid an arranged marriage, flew to America and stayed with the Shaikhs.

Aisha has taken control of her own matchmaking. She asked a boy to prom.

"He lives in Prowa?" she says, stumbling over the city's name. "Peoria? I don't know how to say it!"

Aisha knew the boy from when she lived in Cairo. His family

owns some company and now he goes to high school in Prowa/
Peoria and will be traveling through Chicago on the weekend
of prom. It seemed like an okay arrangement.

Aisha's art teacher walks up and interrupts the prom-
planning. Two other art instructors come to the room and
they spread Aisha's portfolio around the tables and stand back
and stare, hands on chins. Students arrive for class and gather
around the tables too. Everyone is very quiet, for a very long
time. Then someone whispers, *"These are so good,"* as if only
now aware that someone capable of this had been hidden
in their midst this whole time.

Aisha blushes, right foot tucked underneath her left,
looking at the art in front of her, tugging at the bottom
of her shirt with the drawing of the tiger on it.

In the atrium, a class is layering strips of red tape on
the floor. It's a combined physics and art project. They're
constructing a twenty-foot-tall "perfect face." A maintenance
worker hears this and hoots, "Hey, that don't look like me!"

Anais walks past, her perfect face looking a little less perfect
today. Pale, with dark liner under her eyes. Around her slim

neck she has a gold chain, which she is fingering, pulling tight and twisting. She slumps onto a bench.

"Stressed. It's horrible. Tight muscles, severe headaches. I feel broken down. I feel sick, though I'm not." She pauses, hands on throat. "I just want to sleep."

Anais can't decide where to go to college. After a flawless audition, she was accepted into the ballet conservatory at Indiana, the place she always wanted to go. But then she was accepted by NYU.

Making a choice between the programs is tormenting Anais. They're very different: NYU specializes in modern dance, Indiana in classical ballet. NYU lets students choreograph pieces, Indiana is led by master instructors. NYU would give her a huge scholarship, and allow her to live with friends in Manhattan. Indiana would give her instruction more attuned to her strength in ballet, and allow her to live near cows in the Midwest.

Anais says if she could take the Indiana program out of Bloomington and place it in New York she'd do it *like that*.

"It's the hardest decision of my life," she says, hands still on her throat. "I can't concentrate."

Last night she and her father talked until one in the morning. The conversation went nowhere. How do you say no to one of the best ballet conservatories in the country? How do you say no to a scholarship and New York City? The stress of making the decision follows her everywhere, even to the studio.

"When I'm dancing, I'm wondering where I want to *be* with dancing. When I'm in the studio, I think Indiana. When I get home, and talk to friends like Maya, I switch to NYU."

Indecision is eating her up. The stress will get so intense that on the day before Anais must decide, she will fly to New York. Then, there, she will know.

"If you want to be more influential, you got to step your game *up!*" Anthony barks at a friend. It is unnecessary to mention that Anthony is in the cafeteria, in his same seat, leaning against the same wall.

Anthony's friend is wearing an oversized Atlanta Falcons hat over his cornrows, a Chicago Bulls jersey down to his thighs, and red socks up to his knees. He's lying flat on the table next to Anthony, looking upside down at a chorus of admiring girls.

"I don't *care.* Look at this shit. It's a *new style!*" barks the friend from his horizontal position.

The style in question: rubber bands worn around the tops of one's socks. The girls at the table are discussing whether or not this will cut off the circulation to the boy's feet and cause gangrene. Amputation seems probable. Anthony shakes his head at this foolishness, takes a roll of money out of his front pants pocket, and starts counting.

"He look a damn fool," Anthony mutters to himself. When he's finished counting his roll, he puts it away and starts smoothing the silver sticker on his White Sox hat. He's trying to maintain its "freshness."

"When your sticker comes off, time to let the hat go," he says, explaining the not-so-obvious. Anthony is in a grumpy mood. There are other things he's letting go.

"I'm *done* with Payton girls. It's *official.* I got my feelings hurt."

The last few weeks, Anthony was hanging out with a sophomore girl. It took effort, going after school with the girl and her friends to the nearby Popeye's. But now she has a boyfriend, one of the boys that was going with them to Popeye's. Another disappointment.

His report card also came out last week.

"I haven't seen it. . . . All I know is it was bad."

His mother was required to come to Payton to pick it up. She phoned Anthony and told him he was failing everything, then hung up. The odd thing is that Anthony says his classes are not so hard.

"*That* ain't never been a problem. I just don't be *doing* my homework."

When Anthony leaves Payton for the day he doesn't think about school until the following morning. After school is just that. *After school.* Others can study. That's not him. Instead of doing his homework, Anthony smokes weed with one of his cousins, plays basketball with his brother, and eats dinner. Last night Anthony ate a tuna sandwich alone (his mother got a new job at a nursing home and hasn't been around much). Sometimes he watches television.

"I watch *Prison Break* on Mondays. *Lost* on Wednesdays. I don't watch on Tuesdays."

Next week, Anthony's physics class is taking a field trip to Six Flags Great Adventure, but Anthony won't be allowed to go because of his poor grades. His physics teacher, Mr. Dyson, has a rule about that. Anthony says he would like to raise his grades, but . . .

He sneezes. "You gotta *brace* yourself for a sneeze so you don't blow your back out."

Anthony looks around the cafeteria. The friend with the cornrows has left, wrapping up his female admirers and taking them with him. Anthony snorts. It's been a depressing spring, all in all. He takes his money roll out of his pocket and counts it a second time, as if to see whether it's grown. The roll is made up of ones.

MAY

Afternoons are for doodling. Especially in the classrooms with views of downtown. There's so much to get lost in: skyscrapers, airplanes heading east, window-cleaners who look like rock-climbers.

When the teacher's back is turned, a wrapped piece of gum soars across the room. The teacher turns around. He turns back and two girls mouth a conversation across the room.

"Are you going to ————"

"Where?"

"To ————!"

"What?"

"Later."

In the field next to Cabrini Green, a phys ed class is picking tree blossoms. Girls line blossoms on their forearms, or blow them off their palms. A boy hangs from the branch above the girls, flexing his biceps. After he falls to the ground, everyone lurches into the nearby playground to kick some balls. As they do, it seems that what is being learned in phys ed is confidence in the lack of physical confidence, and in this the students play together as if they were a team.

Some students are still keeping up appearances. Daniel, in a red-striped Michael Kors dress shirt, looks especially sharp today. The red shirt matches the rest of the atrium: the red paper lanterns hanging from the balconies, the red banners on the walls, the red papier-mâché dragons guarding the library. Students were told to wear red today for the ceremony commemorating the school's new Chinese Confucius Institute, so Daniel did.

Daniel hasn't been thinking much about not getting into Harvard. Sometimes he wonders if all his extracurriculars may have kept him from his schoolwork. He thinks if he'd done

better in his classes, maybe things would have been different. Those four B's probably didn't help. He sees that now. He says he has no regrets.

Daniel was recently interviewed by the *Chicago Tribune* for an article about outstanding minorities going to outstanding colleges. He's excited about Penn. And today he gets to see the mayor.

The mayor is coming to Payton for the opening of the Confucius Institute, a *thing* within the Chicago public schools funded by the Chinese government. It's not clear what the *thing* is (library, computer room, cultural center for understanding and propaganda), but it has shut down the bathrooms and lockers and stairs at the east end of the atrium. Filling the space are Chinese diplomat types in red scarves, local politicians in suits, and student greeters in red T-shirts.

TV camera lights snap on. Dignitaries step to a podium: the principal, the alderman, the head of the

Chicago public schools, the head of the Confucius Institute in his thick black Mao glasses, the mayor.

As the mayor begins his speech, Daniel listens intently. He thinks, *I can do this*. The public appearances, the meetings, the openings. It gives Daniel motivation, gives him thoughts about his future.

At the other end of the atrium are a group of Payton students, and they are oblivious. They're playing Ping-Pong. They're loud. They have been asked to stop. Their ball-smacking and shouting start making it difficult to hear the mayor. The games are drowning him out. Administrators scurry over to install order but they can't quite.

Daniel doesn't turn his head. Eventually the Ping-Pong uprising is squashed. The ceremony continues. Little speeches, little choreographed moments, little patterings of polite applause—except from Daniel. When the mayor finishes his speech, Daniel claps especially hard.

Since that awful tie with Parker, Emily's team has been playing well and winning games. Emily's sister recovered from her twisted ankle. While she doesn't have Emily's ball skills, she is faster, and has a wicked shot. She's the future.

Today is a big cloud day, and the stands of Winnemac Park on the city's North Side are packed with students and parents. Payton is playing Lane Tech in the semis of the Chicago city tournament. As the second half starts, the game remains scoreless: the type of game that ends with a mistake. If it does, number 13 for Lane Tech will probably have caused it. Number 13 is thin as a blade of grass, and as hard to catch. She has kept the Payton defenders on their heels all day with blazing acceleration and cocky moves. It's a wonder she hasn't scored. Already she's knocked two balls off the goalposts. When she clangs another shot into the post, a penalty shot, even the referee puts his hand to his head. Maybe luck is with Payton today.

The sun begins lowering over the field, and it's pink and very pretty. Then, a mistake. A scuffed clearance that lands at the feet of number 13, who races the length of the field and slides the ball under the Payton goalie. Game over.

Emily is the last player off the field. One of her freshmen tries to comfort her by putting her arm around her shoulder. Emily shakes it off. As their coach talks to them, Emily sits in the stands three rows above her team. Some players are crying. Not Emily. But the game isn't her last. Next week is States.

Maya made her decision. NYU. She's already gotten her NYU e-mail address, she'll be in a great acting studio, she'll be in another studio that studies art by going to Appalachia and playing music and stuff. At this, Maya laughs and cracks her knuckles and flips her bangs, all at the same time.

"I'm really excited!"

Maya just finished eating lunch in of all places the cafeteria. She almost never eats there, as she's one of the seniors who go out for lunch, but today she was late and her friends went without her. Now she's killing time, sitting on a bench in the atrium, listening to a man tune a piano.

The piano is being tuned for some performance later in the week. The tuner starts hitting the low notes, *dong, dong, dong,* and Maya raises one eyebrow at the absurdity of having her words set to a soundtrack.

"*Okay!* I went to work the other day? I was punching numbers into the cash register, and I had a panic attack. Having to listen to the *same* video music playing, punching numbers into a *cash* register. I can't deal with this. Is this me? And then I was, like, *okay.*"

It wasn't bad for one reason. "I think in terms of material. I do that with everything if I'm complaining. If I'm having trouble with someone I can use them as a character."

It's a strategy she finds helpful. Just last week Maya went to a poetry reading. Ms. Murphy told the entire English class to go but only Maya went. There she was, the one person under thirty, everyone around her acting smart and literary, saying *hmmm* at the end of each poem, and the whole thing was so silly she thought about leaving. But after looking at the crowd she stayed and took mental notes, and when she got home she wrote them down.

The same appreciation for the bizarre may help Maya with prom. She's been asked by bunches of boys, none of whom she wants to go with. One even asked her on Facebook.

"I didn't actually respond. I'm pretty much a terrible person! I didn't want to ruin his feelings."

Maya scrunches up her nose. She's decided to go to prom with another friend, a boy she's been friends with since freshman year. She hopes he understands they're going as friends. People have a way of not understanding, though. Like Ben, the ex-boyfriend. Things haven't worked out between them in the amicable way Maya would have wished.

Dee, dee, dee. The tuner starts hitting the high notes.

Maya squints at him, possibly adding another character to her list.

Dee, dee, dee.

"This music is making me nervous," she says. She turns to the tuner and whispers fiercely: "Oh, God. *Stop!*"

The man can't hear. Maya cracks up, and pokes her tongue into her cheek, turning her cheek into her cheek tent.

Maya knows she fidgets, knows she has a whole array of tics. The tongue in cheek, the rolling foot, the hand washing. Her sisters tease her about her tics all the time. Sometimes she thinks she fidgets because it's calming, and then she notices she fidgets even when she's not nervous. Maybe it's just part of who she is, as indelible as a birth mark.

The piano tuner has stopped. Maya gets up to go. She has somewhere she must be. Last week the yearbook came out and Maya had been voted *Most Likely to Be Famous.*

If the atrium is a stage, the bathrooms may be the art house theaters that show the edgier plays. One work-in-progress from the spring season, as yet untitled:

"You sucking your thumb?"

"*Naw.*"

"You got a nosebleed?"

"*Uh.*"

"You better go splash some water on that!"

"*Uh-huh.*"

(The boy with the nosebleed exits.)

"Hey, why'd you hit that boy?"

Diana sits in the field next to the high school, twirling her ID around her forefinger. She's wearing blue gym shorts. Her flip-flops are off. When not twirling her ID, she's ripping blades of grass and piling them on her toes.

"It's nice outside. So I think it's summer!"

Diana has always felt that high school was just one part of her life. Now that part is even smaller. She feels she's in a different world. Last week she only came to school one day. For four *years* she's been going to class, doing homework, volunteering, applying herself. Now that's almost over.

"I've been so thoughtful for so long," she says.

Diana's best friend Sandra runs over and whispers in her ear: Their old friend Suki is going to prom with the cute guy everyone wanted to go to prom with. Sandra runs away.

Diana hasn't told Sandra, but last week she went to a party with Suki. It's not the same as before they had their falling out, but it was nice to see that some part of the friendship survived.

"I have a lot of different friends, and they don't all get along. People have their own opinions. It's always been like that."

Friends are a constant juggling act for Diana. Each group claiming her for their own: friends from the neighborhood who tell Diana she shouldn't act too white, white friends who tell her she shouldn't act too ghetto, other friends. With more free time now, there's more time for drama with her friends. There's even been some tension between Diana and Sandra.

Diana doesn't know who she's going to prom with. She knows she will go with friends, but which ones is a question. She knows her mother will make her dress.

She stops.

Her brother is coming home from jail next week.

"He's going to be on house arrest. I don't know for how long. I feel we're going . . ." Diana pauses and plucks some grass. "I feel it's going to be stressful for all of us. I can see it coming.

"He's going to want to have his friends over."

She starts building the grass into a neat pile.

"He might change."

She adds more grass.

"He might not be able to come to my graduation. He's going to be wearing an ankle brace."

She knocks the pile down. Diana's sisters are still working at the car wash. They complain that they're overweight, but washing cars is the only exercise they get. They say they're going back to school in the fall, but don't know where. Diana will be in Urbana-Champaign, at the University of Illinois. She'll concentrate then. Right now, she wants to have fun.

She has been hanging out more and more with her lifeguard coworkers. They're in their early twenties. She's been going with them to parties and bars. They all watched the recent Oscar de la Hoya boxing match together. Maybe Diana will go to prom with one of them.

The brown line train rumbles by on its tracks.

"I always have to be choosing between friends."

She rips up another handful of grass.

"I want to be by myself."

She throws the grass in the air.

"It's going to be good for me to get away."

Last week, there was a huge march downtown for immigrant rights. Hundreds of thousands of immigrants and their supporters waving banners and flags, marching through the Haymarket and unfurling over the bridges and into the canyons of the Loop, shutting down the city. Diana skipped school to march. But she couldn't persuade her sisters to go. She couldn't persuade her mother. Her father had to work. So, in the end, Diana didn't march, even though she wanted to. She just didn't want to do it by herself.

A pack of kids sit on the benches behind Truman rolling blunts. One of them is Zef. He's not partaking, though. Ten minutes later, at the Starbucks across the street, he's sipping his Americano and laughing, because just as he was leaving, the kids got busted by a teacher.

"I *told* them!" he chuckles.

Zef is smiling but seems out of sorts. There's a girl he likes who doesn't like him back. As he leans in his tight-fitting gray jacket into the Starbucks wall, he starts twirling the white wires of his iPod earphones around his head like a lasso.

"I met this girl named Daisy, and then she just dropped off

the edge of the planet. Really skinny, really short. Reddish-brown hair. Good-looking? *Hell,* yeah."

Zef's earphone wires start twirling faster.

"Everybody calls her Daisy. She wants people to call her Daisy Mae, but they don't," he says, adding, "Her favorite flowers are yellow roses."

Zef hung out with Daisy the last few days, but he doesn't know where she is anymore. He never bothered to get her number. When he mentions this, his earphone wires stop rotating and plonk down onto the table.

"I have a really hard time meeting girls," he admits.

With his lazy good looks, girls usually approach Zef. But what to do if they don't approach is a question he doesn't know how to answer.

"I don't really do anything to meet people," he acknowledges with a shrug. As the Americano kicks in, Zef's mood improves. Also, he's flush with money. He flashes the fifty-Euro note some guy gave him for directing another guy to a third guy who sells 'shrooms. It was good money, but there was a catch. There's always a catch.

"*Currency* exchanges no longer exchange *currency!*" Zef exclaims, laughing at the absurdity of it all. Zef has been making money other ways, though. With his iPod fixed, he's renting out the iPod Nano he was given by his grandmother. He was also given five hundred dollars by relatives for his birthday. And though he lost his wallet a few days after that (he thinks it fell out of his pocket when he was climbing a tree), the five hundred dollars was not inside.

Last week he turned seventeen. Zef celebrated by not going to school. Instead, he went to Payton.

It wasn't because of any affection. "That motto they have? 'We breed leaders,' something like that. But, the drugs! That school is *ridiculous,*" he says, nodding. "It's gone downhill since I left."

Zef met up with his friends at the Payton front door since he is not allowed inside. They went to one of their houses and hung out and then went to Zef's house and hung out. He's been hanging out a lot this month. Last weekend he went to his first rave. He rode in the back of a friend's red convertible, wind whipping through his hair, cruising south on the interstate. The rave was in a bowling alley.

"Too hot in the basement. Everyone dancing. No fan, got real unpleasant. It was a good time."

Zef starts twirling his earphone lasso again. He has plans for summer.

"Get speakers for the car, get my license."

"Go to the beach!" pipes in Zef's friend, the same friend who joined Zef last time, Silent Bob's not-so-silent brother.

"I don't like the beach. I like pools," Zef states, putting an end to that.

Silent Bob's brother takes off someplace. Zef frowns, his mood hopping from glum to animated to glum in a venti-induced heartbeat. Zef hasn't been making much music recently.

"It's kind of like writer's block, but, like, for music."

He hasn't been inspired. He's getting forgetful. Today he forgot to bring his cell phone to school.

"I feel weird without my phone. I feel quite naked," Zef says, patting the empty spot on his belt where the phone usually hangs out. Its absence seems to distract him. He picks up his earphones, twirls them, lets them fall.

"I want a girlfriend," he says. Then he's quiet for a long time.

"I *do* things, know what I'm saying? I should be a lot happier than I am."

Zef reconsiders, picks up his earphones and starts twirling again.

"Things are good. I am. *Yeah.*"

Zef takes a last pull on his coffee, then heads outside. He's still talking, ricocheting from girls to music to sleep to girls. Life can be exhilarating and baffling, often in the exact same moment.

A bus rumbles past: Zef's bus. Off he runs, arms waving like an ostrich trying to gain flight, trying to flag down the bus before it leaves him by the side of the road.

Aisha thinks back to the beginning of the school year when she had no friends. She feels she's made friends since then—the girls from her art class who let her into their group. They're not best friends or anything, but friends. Last weekend they all went out to dinner and then to a chick-flick.

She likes these girls, though she wonders if she'll remember them a few years from now. This was just a year, it was always that. Sometimes she feels bad that she didn't have a classic high school experience, and then she doesn't. She's always been able to pick up and go.

Aisha is sitting in her art teacher's office, wearing a T-shirt with SPEEDWEEK DAYTONA BEACH in garish letters across the front. Her Florida grandmother loves "the NASCAR."

Aisha had her final Arabic class. The class divided into groups and wrote a scene where a girl meets her suitor's family.

"I played the young girl who was getting proposed to," Aisha says, chuckling.

Daniel Patton, in a suit, pokes his head into the art office, waves, pokes his head out. Aisha raises her eyebrows, amused by this awkward and well-dressed interruption.

The cast was made up of Aisha, a girl from Yemen, and two Spanish "kids." One of the "kids" is a Spanish professor at Loyola University. He kept screwing up his lines.

"He'd jump in two pages after he was supposed to and say 'Your mother is from Jordan!' And we're like, 'That's not your cue!'"

Aisha wipes her eyes, she's laughing so hard. Her art teacher pops her head in. She needs the office.

Aisha heads into the halls, walking past the lockers and the trophy cases, looking for the sets she helped paint for the spring play. She drops her pencil. As she bends to pick it up, she starts talking about her family. Her father got a new engineering job in Austin, Texas. The Shaikhs will relocate again, though her sisters will stay in Chicago to finish their next year of school. Aisha wishes the family would buy a house in Chicago and move the family's possessions up from Florida. They need space to keep all the things they've accumulated from their travels around the world.

"And I'm not just talking a stool. Antique stuff from China. All teak and heavy," Aisha says, furrowing her brow. "What are we going to do with it?"

She stops. A physics class is running an experiment in the hallway in front of her, two wheeled metal cars bouncing headlong into each other before bouncing back.

Aisha wonders what she would put in the *Important Box* now, what she would take with her next year to college. But there's no answer really, no *thing* that she would miss. Some things can't be packed neatly in a box. Every now and then, on the weekend, Aisha smokes a *shisha* water pipe with her father. She will miss that.

It's the state quarterfinals, Payton girls' soccer against Lane Tech, the same team they lost to in the city semifinals. All eyes in Lane Tech's stadium are on Lane's number 13, the blade of grass with the bold moves who single-handedly beat Payton last time. When she has the ball, fans in the Payton stands yell, "She's *too dangerous!*"

Number 13 has almost 40 goals this year, 150 over her career. That's why, today, the only thing that Emily is doing is marking her. Wherever number 13 goes, Emily goes. One foot behind her. One hand on her jersey, sacrificing her position as the best player on her team to stop the best player on the other team (and sacrificing any chance for Payton to score).

Even with Emily's attention, there are times when number 13 gets the ball, with Emily draped over her, and turns and rips a shot that skims over the crossbar. Emily is playing someone better than she.

At the end of regulation, the game is tied. The first overtime brings nothing. The second overtime brings more nothing.

The game comes down to penalty kicks. If Payton loses, their season is over. Emily crouches off to the side, watching what could be the last moment of her high school soccer career.

The teams start shooting and Emily chews her nails. She throws her arm around her sister, who crouches beside her with her jersey pulled over her face because she can't look. As the shoot-out continues it becomes clear that Emily will not shoot. Her freshmen will. When one misses,

Emily shuffles over and hugs her. And when one makes the shot that wins the game, Emily leads the rest of her team in a mad sprint across the field to lift her into the air.

Anais Blake doesn't really have to be at school anymore, but she has an errand she needs to take care of. She glides through the front door wearing a flippy skirt, sunglasses, and small sandals with flowers across the straps.

She is not as carefree as her clothes. While other seniors are ditching school to go to the beach, Anais is dancing at the studio. And, scooping ice cream. She started working at an Italian ice place near her home. She's learning the art of the scoop, how to serve frozen yogurt.

"I'm still not perfect at that swirly thing," she says with a delicate turn of her wrist. She doesn't know how long she'll work this summer, probably until sometime in August when she heads off to Bloomington, to Indiana University.

Anais made her decision to attend Indiana when she flew to New York. She walked into a dance studio at NYU and just *knew*. It wasn't good enough. Arty yet not artistic. Hello, Indiana.

And yet, making the decision has not lessened Anais's stress.

She has so many friends going to New
York, including Maya. She worries
if her decision is the right one,
giving the impression that worry is something that will always
be with her, like an extra bone in her foot.

Anais's ankles are stronger now, though her feet are blis-
tered. With her sandals, the blisters are easier to see: a gaping
red one on her left big toe, a nasty little one on her right heel.
Anais was voted *Biggest Klutz* in the yearbook, though that was
probably intended to be ironic.

"The more I think about it, the more I want to be in a company," she says as she slides along the hallway. Last month,
Anais tried to audition for the Joffrey Ballet but was informed
there were no openings. The woman told Anais she was still
young, to audition next year. That was small consolation.

"Young is like sixteen."

Timing is everything in dance. Next year Anais will
audition for the Joffrey, and if they accept her she would
leave college in a second. Good-bye, Indiana.

Over the weekend, Anais had her final performance
with the Civic Ballet of Chicago. The Ruth Page Center
auditorium was packed. In the first piece, Anais danced a

classic *pas de deux* in a white tutu. In her last piece Anais wore a black one-piece with a blue stripe down the side. The piece was modern and edgy, choreographed by a professional from Hubbard Street Dance. The dancers were slithering all over the floor.

Anais stood out. She was strong, her line sure and precise, the most poised dancer except for the twenty-something professional from Hubbard Street. As she leaped across the stage, all the pain and stress melted away, and the love she felt for dance was clear. The smile on her face was radiant, so radiant it could almost fool someone watching into thinking that what she was doing was not difficult. Onstage, she had grace.

Clothes have come full circle. For boys, new faded T-shirts from Abercrombie & Fitch. For girls, an even more economical use of fabric, accessorized with wide belts, flip-flops, and fat sunglasses.

In one morning advisory, a group of girls gather in a corner to discuss the details of tonight's party.

"Is there going to *be* an after-party?"

"Sure."

"How sure?"

Their voices grow more hushed as they figure out who will bring the refreshments. They get louder when figuring out who is going.

"Will is going!"

"Will is going?"

"Will is *going*."

"Clare is going!"

"Clare is going?"

"Clare is . . . "

The bell rings and the girls stream into the halls. One dips into the bathroom. She comes out a minute later but forgot something, stopping to look in the reflected glass of the trophy case to check her hair and adjust her bra strap.

Anthony sits by himself in the cafeteria. He has no arms. It takes a second to see that they are under his tan *Drunken Monkey* T-shirt, his fingers occasionally appearing at the shirt's bottom like little animals poking their noses out of a cave.

Most juniors are studying for finals. Not Anthony. He's getting an F in precalculus, an F in literature, an F in Afro American history. He has to write extra papers just to get

D's, but whether or not that will happen is an open question.

Things happen *to* Anthony, not the other way around. Last week he went to a party and had a smoke and then went to McDonald's, but somewhere along the way he lost his money roll and his bus pass, so he had to talk his way onto the "L" and once he got home he realized he still had two bags of weed in the pockets of his shirt.

His father asked why he was late. Anthony made up some story, which his father didn't believe. As he hurried to his room, his father asked about the bulges in his shirt pockets, so Anthony started running. Darting into his room, his father close behind, he slipped one bag of weed into a sock, the other into a college envelope (he stashes drugs there because he figures that's the last place his parents would look).

His father found the pot in his sock. They can't punish Anthony, though. They have his phone, his iPod. They have his driver's license, which he got last week but which is staying in his father's wallet until his grades improve.

"They've taken away all that they can take away," Anthony says, hands jammed inside his pants. Anthony is broke despite the fact that he is still selling drugs. He runs through money quick. A shirt, a movie, some food, then it's gone. Maybe he'll get a job.

"I want to work at Foot Locker," Anthony says, nodding.

He also wants to get in shape. He says he's going to try out for the football team in the fall. He's going to play wide receiver.

Can he make the team?

"Yeah, that's not a problem. I just gotta get recognized."

How good is he?

"I'm *real* good," he continues, yawning. "I *was* real good."

Anthony last played in eighth grade. While he talks, The Girl walks into the cafeteria and up to Anthony's table. She's wearing a tight pink and red striped shirt that cannot conceal the fact that she is very, very pregnant.

"Hi, Anthony!" She smiles, waving down at him.

Anthony makes eye contact with her but does not say a word. She stays a moment, keeps walking. A minute passes.

"We basically stopped . . . " He doesn't finish. "I care less and less every time I see that now." He pauses.

"The whole situation. That was tough for me. I learned a lot from that. I learned about relationships in general. A freshman guy said to me he's going to be with his girl forever. But eventually *she's* going to do something to *him*. He going to do something to *her*. Eventually, you going to *learn*."

He yawns again. He says he is looking forward to senior year.

"I'm trying to improve upon everything."

Another minute passes.

"This has been a long year. *This has been a long year,*" he says. Then, apropos of not much, he says, "I brought this upon myself. Ain't no point going through stuff if you can't learn from it."

He nods and puts his arms back through his sleeves, slaps the table, and gets up to go. The situation is what it is.

JUNE

Daniel was woken this morning by his father banging a broomstick on the ceiling from the apartment downstairs. All spring Daniel has been waking up to the alarm on his Treo, when it works. When it doesn't, the broomstick.

After showering and dressing, Daniel lopes out the front door. The brick houses of the South Side stand quiet, the lawns wet with dew. The dilapidated corner store is still locked. No one is up this early except the birds. The bus trundles into view. Daniel slides into a seat in the back, stretching his long legs. Watching other commuters board in their spring clothes he murmurs, "Nothing better than wearing nice soft colors."

Daniel himself is wearing dress pants, a striped shirt, white sneakers, and a recently purchased silver Kenneth Cole watch. Daniel was voted *Best Dressed* in the yearbook. He pulls out his Treo and starts clicking through photos from another high school's prom that he went to: Daniel and his date, Daniel and his cake, Daniel and his date eating cake. He has been thinking about his own prom too. He had been planning to fly in a girl from California whom he met while visiting Penn. It was turning into a logistical nightmare, though: how to get her hair done, her nails done, then fly her back, all in one day.

Daniel asked Emily instead. They're going as friends, that's all. The arrangement is convenient for him, as he won't have to entertain anybody.

"That's where she lives," he says, nodding out the window as the brownstones of Hyde Park slide past.

As the bus lurches up along the lake, the skyscrapers of downtown shimmer into view, and Daniel talks about how he's been making this ride for years. Four years of high school. All the hours, all the work, all the rides, everything propelling him to college and beyond. And these are the last times he'll take this ride. It makes him nostalgic. The bus passes the lion statues in front of the Art Institute, and turns into the Loop.

Daniel gets on the subway and rides north to Division, emerging at the Dunkin' Donuts. He buys two croissants (a step up from last fall's bagel), heads west on Division Street, turns left on North Wells, and walks through the front door of school, only a few minutes late.

When he was sitting on the bus looking up at the buildings of downtown, Daniel talked about how he has changed since the fall. He thinks he's become more of a capitalist. Worrying about financial aid was a factor. Even though scholarships and his parents will pay for much of his college tuition, money remains a concern.

After college, he needs to make a lot of money. To pay off debt, to support his lifestyle, to fund a campaign if he runs for office. Not for representative, though. Daniel no longer wants to be a congressional representative, even one as charismatic as Barack Obama. What he really wants to be is a mayor. Running a city, like Chicago.

When Daniel met the mayor recently he told him just that, that someday he means to have his job. He has a signed photograph from that meeting:

To Daniel Patton. Best Wishes, Mayor Richard M. Daley.

———

The five pleasant days of spring in Chicago have come and gone. It's summer now, oppressive and hot. A group of students sits outside the front door throwing ice at each other.

Inside school it's stuffy. White Sox signs from the fall slump off the walls in the humidity. Students lounge around the atrium signing yearbooks, flipping through the pages to see what others wrote. One girl has a stack of yearbooks next to her, assembly-line style.

"Want me to sign your yearbook?"

"No. Fuck you."

"Heh, heh."

"See you!"

Only underclassmen are at school, waiting to take finals. As they wait they watch the Ping-Pong, hands in pockets, heads going back and forth. The King of Ping-Pong is king again. The underclassmen look taller than they were in the fall— in some cases an inch or two—but also bigger in personality, a larger amount of confidence to fill the space of those that will soon leave.

At the front door the security

guard reads the *Sun-Times,* waving kids in,  barely looking up. A biology class is running a frog race. The contestants just sit there at first.

"Your frog a loser! Your frog a *loser!*" one student taunts.

Then the frogs are poked in their bottoms and start leaping. Not where they are supposed to—the finish line near the trophy cases—but across the linoleum toward the exit and freedom. The only ones in the high school making any effort anymore are frogs, and even they are trying to get out the door.

Emily walks through the atrium, her hair no longer in a tight ponytail but in a wild mane of curls, bouncing as if a weight had been lifted from her.

"I have a craving. It's very serious. I need nachos!" she calls out.

With that, Emily pushes through the door and strides across the field to the parking lot. She gets in her shimmery green Honda Civic (voted *Best Car* in the yearbook) and accelerates through the small streets around the high school, heading downtown. Her windows are down, and the wind whips through her hair and around the car and up to the tops of the steel buildings that rise on either side of her. When Emily reaches her destination, she double-parks, leaps out, and shuffles to the taqueria.

Five minutes later and Emily is back, goal accomplished, nachos in hand. She throws the bag on the floor of the passenger seat, and speeds back through downtown. She's wearing a T-shirt from the Broadway show *Wicked*. It says *defy gravity* across the chest. After first seeing *Wicked* in the winter, Emily has seen it five more times. She thinks *Wicked* is the best show ever.

"*So* amazing!" she cries.

Emily fell in love with the music, fell in love with the story. Emily changes lanes, and subjects.

"My friends are annoying," she snaps.

Some of Emily's friends were upset with her this spring because she was so caught up with her soccer team. Meanwhile, they were sitting around talking about boys and doing not much else. Emily is looking forward to meeting people in college who are more like her, more willing to talk about serious issues. She's thinking of trying out for the women's soccer team at Yale. Her Payton coach thinks she's good enough. Over the summer she'll play with a traveling team to improve her game, and her shot.

Emily parks her Honda and sips her drink—the cup says *Eat the World* on its side—and starts walking across the field back to school. With schoolwork over, Emily has had time to experiment with her own writing. She started a fiction piece, and a dream journal. And, she has a new crush.

"No one can ever know that I like him," she says, green eyes flashing.

Emily pushes through the front door. As she heads down the halls, swinging her right shoulder, then her left, she talks about how her goals from the beginning of the year have not changed. She still wants a job in business. She still wants money, still wants power. The thought of someday going to work in a suit makes her happy.

"This is *who I am,*" she says.

Emily stops.

When her team lost in the state semifinals, it was hard. They lost to St. Ignatius, who lost to New Trier, who then won it all. The team didn't accomplish Emily's goal of making it to finals. Emily doesn't feel she accomplished *her* goals either, though she was still All-City, All-Conference, All-Section, and won all sorts of other awards.

Emily feels St. Ignatius wasn't better than Payton, they were just more confident. She made dumb decisions, passing to teammates who were open but who she knew wouldn't be able to do anything with the ball once they got it. She marked the other team's best player again, taking out her own team's chances of scoring. She didn't shoot. She moved forward at the end, though by then the game was over.

As the minutes counted down, Emily felt increasingly emotional. With one minute left she called to a teammate to pass the ball back to her so she could touch it one last time before her season ended, and then she choked up and cried.

Emily doesn't say anything. She looks down the hallway, done talking about this last moment in her career as a soccer player, this moment that made her tear up, if only briefly, alone on a field in a game that had embraced her for her whole life. It's an admission both surprising and sweet.

Then Emily sees one of her teammates, takes off her own ID and throws it at her, hitting her smack in the rear end.

The last day of school, nothing more to do. In Ms. Murphy's English class, six students have shown up, seven if you count the one napping on the couch that has magically appeared outside the classroom door. Maya is somewhere outside, lying in the sun and eating an apple.

"What are we doing today?" asks a student in a T-shirt with RELAX on its front.

"Option A is watch a movie," says Ms. Murphy, bouncy as ever. "Option B is go outside and tie ribbons on trees!"

Option B it is.

The class heads outside with Ms. Murphy, due in August, waddling in front. They start tying ribbons on trees to raise awareness of the genocide in Darfur, though the boys think the real purpose of tying ribbons on trees is to hug as many girls as possible.

"*Mmm*. Your hair is so fragrant," says the skinny boy with the big ears as he envelops the prettiest girl in the class. He's hugging everyone, but mostly her. After half an hour of "ribbon tying," the class heads back inside. A girl sees a friend and peels off to tell her something. A boy leaves to play hacky sack. A girl heads to the bathroom. The class dissolves into particles and into molecules and then into nothing. Ms. Murphy, walking to her room, turns and sees that no one is with her.

"What happened to my class?"

From the insulated second floor of the Drake Hotel, a hard summer wind can be seen whipping down Michigan Avenue. Tourists lean into the gusts, clutching their shopping bags. On Lake Shore Drive, car lights blink against a dark blue sky. And

inside the Drake, under the gilded chandeliers and twenty-foot-tall mirrors of the Gold Coast Room, the Payton senior class prom is in full swing.

Students whirl around looking shiny. Boys in tails and vests and bowler hats. Girls in tight dresses, bright as M&M'S. Everyone leaning toward digital cameras. As always, the girls

are experiencing problems with engineering—high-heel break-downs, spaghetti-strap malfunctions—and heading to the bathroom for repairs.

Daniel and Emily swoop past not holding hands, he looking elegant in black tails, she looking uncomfortable in a dress. Diana is on the dance floor with one of her lifeguard coworkers.

Aisha sits at a back table with her date from Prowa/Peoria, a little smile on her face. Anais shuffles past in a slender green dress, Maya clutching her arm. They're laughing. They've both ditched their dates. The boy from Minnesota couldn't come. Ben&Andy decided not to come either.

After all the talk surrounding prom—who was going with whom, what everyone was wearing, how they were getting there, where they were going before, when they were arriving exactly, why was she *really* going with him—the most exciting part of prom *was* the talk. As the students sit around the ballroom on upholstered chairs, sipping at glasses of melting ice, stumbling onto the floor for a dance, the night becomes anticlimactic. Is this it? Yes, it is.

Despite this, everyone's talking about the parties after prom.

Mr. Dyson struts across the field next to the school. He's wearing plaid pants, pointy leather shoes, a puffy paisley hat, and water goggles. On top of this getup he's wearing a graduation robe. If there were a high school for pimps, and they had commencement, Mr. Dyson could be the valedictorian.

As he swaggers across the field, students stare.

"I *dare* ya'll to dunk me!" Mr. Dyson croons. "Who wants some!"

Most students do. They file behind him pied piper style, drawn by the fact that a good teacher can also be cool. Well, not that cool.

"My name is *The Untouchable,* baby!" he bellows at the now sizable crowd gathered around him, before mounting the seat of the dunk tank and being dropped into the water with one of the first throws.

It's field day. Around the field are tables with ice cream, tables with donuts, the dunk tank, a stage with the second-place act from the talent show. In the middle of the field are games of volleyball, bocce, and soccer. Anyone not playing is running around squirting water on other people's shirts.

Walking across the field, floating above the silliness, is Maya. She's wearing leather sandals and jeans, a low-cut green top. A blue band holds back her hair. She looks almost sophisticated, older than even a week ago. She's debriefing with some friends about prom.

"Who dressed you?" she jokes. Maya herself wore a light blue dress from BCBG. The friends agree that prom was fun, but not too fun. There were the usual dramas: a limo that never came, a corsage that fell apart. As the girls talk, a small boy walks up and asks Maya to sign his yearbook.

"I'll catch you *later*," she says, in jokey celebrity mode, flashing him a bright smile. He shrinks away.

After prom, Maya and Anais and other friends went to somebody's house. The girls danced. The boys didn't. In the morning the somebody's parents made everyone breakfast. No one slept.

Maya's friends head off across the field to get something to drink. She talks about the upcoming months. Over the summer she will work at Nordstrom and at the Lookingglass Theatre. In the fall, she will fly to New York and NYU. She will audition for plays, audition for films. She can't wait.

Her entire year has brought her to this: a feeling that is almost overwhelming, building with anticipation, swelling with the knowledge that the opportunities of the world will soon be laid in front of her. Tomorrow is almost here. Who knows, someday she will star in that movie she's always dreamed about, with Wes Anderson directing.

And with that, Maya sticks her tongue into her cheek and laughs.

A summer storm kicks up from the west, whipping dirt into the air and turning the afternoon dark. On Pulaski Avenue on the city's West Side, cars have turned on their lights. In the backyard of the Martinez home, tables are moved to the garage, containers of food carried under the lee of the garage's roof, beach umbrellas folded down. Diana's graduation party may be in some danger.

As everyone waits for the storm's inevitable arrival, Diana's mother keeps handing out the plates of beef and rice and salsa she spent the whole week cooking. Diana's beaming father keeps serving bottles of beer and *Jarritos* soft drinks. Diana's sisters sit around. Diana's little brother chases Diana's nephew under the tables. Diana's older brother, back from jail and busting out of a white tank top with a cigarette behind each ear, lifts visitors off the ground with back-thumping hugs. The family eats and listens to the Mexican dance music pumping like thunder. In the middle of all this commotion, Diana plays host, her smile never leaving her face for an instant.

She takes visitors for a tour of her house: the family room and kitchen, the apartment she shares with her sisters, the bedroom where her bed touches three of the room's walls, the aquarium with the turtle squatting motionless in a pool of water.

"Yes," she says, the word coming out with none of the tentativeness from earlier in the year. "That's a small snapping turtle."

Diana walks back to the yard. The wind has died down, the storm has passed over.

Later that evening, Diana's older brother wants some of his friends to come to the party. The rest of the family does not. Diana negotiates with her mother, trying to prevent an explosion. Then her lifeguard friends show up, along with friends from the neighborhood, along with friends from high school. They all sit at separate tables.

Diana walks back and forth, smiling and trying to keep everyone happy. As she makes her way between the tables—a part of this group, apart from that group—it's clear that navigating the shoals of these waters will never be easy.

Next year can't come too soon.

Downtown, the Harris Theater. Parents with flowers, grandparents with camcorders, siblings with no desire to be here. Everyone dressed up and looking good except for the odd uncle wearing a Cubs hat. It's come to this: graduation.

The concert band starts "Pomp and Circumstance" but the families don't stop talking. If anything, they talk louder so they can be heard over the music. Then the soon-to-be-graduates march in, wearing around their necks orange hoods so bright that if they all wanted to work alongside the interstate after the ceremony they could. They jam the aisles, waving at the crowd. Someone shouts, *"Adrienne!"* The Payton faculty saunters in their colorful hoods, boards worn at goofy angles. Commencement commences.

Maya calmly leads the crowd in the Pledge of Allegiance. Daniel shouts out some welcoming words. Diana introduces a segment on courage. Then, for what seems like an entire year, everyone endures the twenty-five speakers, five songs, one video, a mind-numbing mess of affirmation. Truisms, wrapped around anecdotes, wrapped around maxims. Words like *purpose* said so many times that the word becomes meaningless, said so many times in fact that it starts sounding funny: "Purpose, purpose, purpus, purpes, porpis, porpoise."

Everyone in the theater is waiting for graduation to distill down to the one moment they came here for: their classmate, their friend, their son, their daughter, walking across the stage, a walk as short as the years of school have been long, to gather a diploma and then to keep going to the other side and quickly, slowly, joyfully, painfully out of their lives: Anais Blake. Maya

Boudreau. Emily Harris. Diana Martinez. Daniel Patton. Aisha Kamillah Shaikh.

So let's leave these students now too. Leave them to their next chapter of who knows what. Leave them to change into whatever shape they choose or have chosen for them. And let's go back to the high school, back to where they started.

Two days after graduation, a trickle of underclassmen have come to Payton to pick up grades or drop off a book, to walk through the hallways past the trophy cases, the orange and blue banners, then back outside to friends waiting in cars still running.

"You gotta do anything else?"

"No."

The building is quiet. Classrooms empty, lockers open, bulletin boards stripped clean, all showing that few things are as empty as an empty hallway at the end of a school year.

And yet, it is within these silent halls that the school waits for all that will come. For the students who will come in the next months, in the next years, in the next decades and beyond. All those students, all those years, ready to begin again.

EPILOGUE

six months later

Daniel Patton is not involved in student government at Penn, though he is friends with the freshman class president. He helped run his campaign.

Daniel has decided to major in communication/commerce, with a minor in consumer psychology, and another minor in Africana studies. He's taking a class with the renowned Professor Michael Eric Dyson, which he's found especially illuminating. He tried out for an

August Wilson play, and though he didn't get a part, he's helping with the show.

Daniel's thirteenth-floor dorm room looks over South Philly. His closet holds twenty pairs of shoes. He hasn't been dressing up in college as much as he did in high school, though. He took a class that made him conscious about branding. And, no cash flow means no new clothes. When Daniel wakes at 10:30 he throws on a T-shirt and some jeans.

Over homecoming weekend there was a fashion show. Daniel took that opportunity to dress up, putting on his gray suit, a crisp white shirt, white Lacoste sneakers. At the after-party, there was lots of dancing and Daniel drank a Long Island iced tea and woke up the next morning with the biggest hangover of his life. It was a fantastic evening.

Daniel has been strategizing about where he will be once he graduates, three years from now. He's on the board of the Black Wharton Undergraduate Association, and in that capacity has been planning the association's conference, meeting representatives of corporations that come through town, networking future opportunities.

Daniel is still open to being mayor of Chicago.

———

Emily Harris did not try out for the soccer team at Yale.

Her senior season at Payton had been so intense, the responsibility so weighty, she just needed a break from soccer. "Didn't want to have anything to do with it," she says. College was a big adjustment for her. There were a couple of evenings in the fall she spent crying on the phone with her mother. It was hard being apart from family, hard starting over.

But she instantly felt more open and intimate with friends in college. They were intellectually surprising and inspiring, the kind of people she had hoped she'd meet when she decided to go to Yale.

Emily's top-floor suite has a view of the trees on Old Campus. It also has a huge red couch, her contribution. She's been enjoying her classes, though it was a bit of a surprise to realize she would have to work.

Emily has become friends with one girl on the women's soccer team, and has a crush on a guy on the men's team. She hasn't acted on it. "I wouldn't know what to do," she says. Other students hook up, sometimes on her red couch. Emily would rather have a relationship.

Emily may still play club soccer at Yale. She says she's out of shape, but doesn't look it.

Over the summer she saw *Wicked* many more times. She won't admit how many. She got to know the show's lead, and was invited backstage. In the fall she went into New York, and through connections, met some Broadway producers. Emily still thinks about acquiring money and power. If she does, she would love to be a Broadway producer.

During the fall Emily wrote a small play, which she sent to her sisters for fun. Next semester she's taking a class in musical theory. She started composing a musical. She's already written one song, which is very pretty.

Maya Boudreau loves New York. She loves NYU. She loves her two roommates—one from Wisconsin, one from London by way of India. They're smart and caring, invested in each other's lives. She didn't expect leaving home to be so easy.

Maya loves her theater study class, her essay writing class, her African dance class, her movement class, her acting class in which she performed a monologue from Adam Rapp's *Stone Cold Dead Serious* about a girl who ran away from home.

Maya has found time to act in a few student films,

and next year will audition for more. She's discovering a deeper attraction for film, and for writing. She's still a little obsessed with Wes Anderson.

In the fall Maya saw "Mr. Big" from *Sex in the City* walking around her neighborhood. He was really tall. She hasn't run into Jonathan Safran Foer, but wouldn't mind if she did.

Maya has been sort of seeing two guys. One plays piano, one plays saxophone. She and the saxophone player have been a couple on-and-off, and can't decide if they're friends, or more.

Ben, the high school boyfriend, also attends NYU. He lives in Maya's dorm, a few floors down. They don't talk much. He has a girlfriend, and a mustache.

Maya still has bangs.

She's been fidgeting in her sleep, which she knows because her smart and caring roommates filmed her while she slept and showed her the clip. Her hands were stroking the air, sort of like she was playing the harp. This cracks her up. Maya has developed another tic as well: an elephant seal–like bark that burbles up inside her. She can't help it. She says, "I hope it stops, because what if it doesn't?"

Every day feels like a wonder to Maya. Walking down Broadway on the way to the studio, the streets of the Village bustling around her, each moment filling with untold possibility. She thinks, *This is where I belong.*

Diana Martinez is happy being away from home. The University of Illinois has the reputation as a big party school, but Diana hasn't gone to many parties. She parties when she's home in Chicago. Living in Urbana-Champaign is "more relaxful."

Diana began the year in temporary housing. Then her roommates left and she had the suite to herself. She enjoys her classes. Her favorite is sociology. She's getting good grades. She's swimming. She often talks on the phone with Sandra, up at DePaul. Sometimes she texts Suki, down at Tulane. More than a few times her boyfriend has come down to visit.

Diana started going out with the boyfriend in the summer. He's a lifeguard friend's boyfriend's brother. He's twenty. He works at a warehouse in Chicago. He lives alone—his family has fallen apart—and seeing the toughness of his life opened Diana's eyes. It made her appreciate her own family, the fact that at least they're all together.

Diana's sisters are no longer working at the car wash. They

work at the day-care center where Diana used to work. Her older brother isn't working, though he has a new baby with a different woman from the mother of his first child. The two women don't know about each other. Diana finds the drama frustrating.

Over the summer, Diana's father got his U.S. citizenship. Diana went with him to pick up his passport. She still translates correspondence when she's home, most recently some forms for her sisters, who want to open a day-care center in the house.

Diana is starting a new job in the admissions office of the business graduate school. A Latina woman in the department will be mentoring her.

Diana still has her nose stud.

Eventually she wants to go to law school. Her boyfriend wants her to transfer to the University of Illinois at Chicago, so she can be closer to him and to home. People have a way of pulling her back to Chicago. But Diana thinks she'll stay where she is in Urbana-Champaign. She says, "I like to finish what I start."

Aisha Kamillah Shaikh has a loony roommate. The roommate didn't do laundry for the first months, building a pile of clothes in the middle of their floor. Then the roommate insisted on placing her bed on top of Aisha's, and woke every morning by hitting her forehead into the ceiling. Then the roommate got the idea of buying an office-size water cooler for the room. Aisha's attitude was to let the roommate do these things, that eventually she'd learn.

Moving was easy for Aisha because she's moved so much. Despite the roommate, or because of the roommate, she likes Claremont. She especially enjoys her Chinese language class. She's not taking art classes, but has sent her mother some elaborately decorated cards.

In Pasadena it is hot during the day, and freezing at night. Aisha wears a red hoodie from the skateboard company Independent, a Palestinian *keffiyeh* around her neck that once was red and white but now has faded into a sort of peach. She almost never wears Pumas. She wears flip-flops now.

Aisha has made a few friends but doesn't love her classmates. She was surprised when some suitemates were critical of her fasting during Ramadan. She likes visiting her brother at Harvey Mudd. His friends are nerdy, but confident in their nerdiness. They've rigged their suite with televisions and an

Xbox, and have started a business turning refrigerators into kegerators.

Aisha hasn't dated, though she was set up with a twenty-two-year-old French exchange student on a "screw your roommate" date. They had a nice evening, though much of what they said was lost in translation.

She enjoyed her trip to Pakistan over the summer. The cousin's wedding was strict and religious. No music, no dancing. Afterward the family flew to Islamabad and stayed in the mountains in a house on stilts. They rented a bus and drove on a twisty road and went goose-hunting. Aisha shot a balloon tied to a tree.

A fortune-teller in Pakistan told Aisha she would marry at twenty-six. Her father just wants her to have children, and has been joking that he would take care of them. Aisha thinks she'll go to law school, though sometimes she plays with the idea of art school.

Over the holidays, she walked into the Abercrombie & Fitch store near the Shaikhs' home in Chicago and was offered a job. She had the *look*. Ethnic, pretty. The *new* look, actually. The company has been hiring diverse-looking salespeople to join their blond-looking salespeople (a lawsuit has been helping them). They want their workers to look American, but what is that?

So Aisha has a temporary job at Abercrombie & Fitch. She finds the whole thing hilarious.

Zef Calaveras took a course in DJ-ing over the summer. It was a fun time. For the final project the students compiled a complete set of house music.

Zef has been playing with his mixing board until midnight on most nights. He sleeps better than he did before, though sometimes he doesn't. He's been taking Ambien, but he just ran out and needs to refill his subscription.

Zef hasn't been late to school this year.

After classes at Truman, Zef spends his free time listening to music on his Nano. Its inferior warranty is "ridiculous." He has a new cell phone, which he found in a taxi. He hasn't changed the ring tone from that of its previous owner.

Zef has a new tan jacket he bought for seven dollars at a thrift store. He also has a new keychain, and longer sideburns. He has the same floppy hair and pillowy good looks. His skin is clearer. His allergies aren't as bad.

The girl he liked named Daisy disappeared. He hasn't met anybody else. His girlfriend from Payton dropped out, and transferred to Truman. They don't talk.

Zef won't graduate from high school in the winter as planned, but he hopes to graduate in June. Next year he wants to attend Columbia College, a small arts college in Chicago that specializes in media and technology.

Zef's favorite drink is still the six shot, half-decaf, no water, iced venti Americano.

Anais Blake did not end up going to college. After a summer of working at the local Italian ice place ("The worst thing a dancer could have done!"), she flew to Miami to study with the Cuban Classical Ballet. She had been going there over the summer to work with their instructor, and when the time came for Anais to head to Indiana, she decided she needed to concentrate entirely on her dancing.

It's been intense. She dances with the company from ten in the morning into the evening. Her ankles are okay, though she's often sore. The only day she does not dance is Sunday. In her spare time she swims, though not at the beach.

It was more intense at the beginning, when Anais lived in the instructor's house with the other dancers: everyone watching dance videos when they weren't dancing, noting what everyone else was eating. Anais even went on a diet.

So she moved into her own apartment with another dancer, a fifteen-year-old. Anais is sort of taking care of her. They go grocery shopping in Anais's air-conditionless Toyota. The other dancers in the group are skilled, but young. They ask Anais what high school was like. That she went to high school is something they find exotic.

It has been hard not having her family around. There are no friends to talk to, no one to date. She's been lonely.

In October, Anais flew to New York and visited Maya. She had a wonderful time. Maya's roommates were fun. Anais talks with Maya on the phone often, and feels they may be even closer now.

Her plan is to audition for the Joffrey Ballet, and other ballet companies, in the spring. Anais wishes she could have jumped from high school straight into a professional company, but she feels that the instruction she's getting now is preparing her to make that leap. She says, "I want to do this. I want to dance."

Anais could still enroll in Indiana. In dance, things change fast. A few months from now Anais could be anywhere.

Anthony Johnson Jr. went out for the football team his senior year at Payton. He wasn't allowed to play in the first games because of barely passing grades from his junior year, and when he played he didn't play much. He backed up on defense.

One play from the season stood out.

Late in some loss, the other team ran a reverse. As Anthony chased the runner, one blocker hit his legs, another slammed into his chest. He was pancaked, and missed the tackle. He remembers lying on the ground, looking up at the blue sky. But then he got up and kept running. His hip hurt for weeks afterward, but he says, "I never quit."

Something changed in Anthony over the summer. He saw there were two roads in front of him. One was the spiraling road he was on, the other a more focused road he was not on. Anthony decided to take the focused road. The structure of football practices helped. He had to show up every day. He couldn't go two days one week, three the next. He also had a job over the summer, working in an "intern situation" at the community paper in his neighborhood.

"I'm not a completely different person. I'm still me," Anthony says. He still hangs out at the back of the cafeteria, in the same seat, in fact. His grades are still bad, though better than before. He worries about graduating. But his perspective has changed, sometimes in small ways. Because he's on the football team, he now knows boys who are white and says hello to them in the halls.

Another development is that The Girl is no longer at Payton. She gave birth to twins. She calls Anthony and asks him to take her out, but he's not interested.

He says he's no longer smoking, that he quit dealing drugs. He got his iPod back and he's waiting for a cell phone. On the weekends he's been driving his mother's Mustang. His mustache is thicker, his voice deeper. He has a new black winter coat.

With his mother's help, Anthony wrote down a list of goals. At its top was: *Live a comfortable life*. Other goals were to work hard, be on time, graduate. Anthony is applying to black colleges in the South, some smaller colleges in Illinois.

He thinks that last year he put everything else in his life in front of school. The Girl, the drugs, the getting caught with drugs, the clowning around in the cafeteria. "Never did more than was necessary," he says.

But things changed. He says he's trying to stay calm-headed. All in all, he's having an okay time in his senior year of high school.

ACKNOWLEDGMENTS

First and foremost, thank you to the eight students: Daniel, Emily, Maya, Diana, Anais, Aisha, Anthony, and Zef, for letting me tag along and ask questions about their lives even as they unfolded. Their openness made this book possible. Thanks also to the rest of the student body, for tolerating a guy with a sketchbook hanging around their hallways and classrooms.

Thanks to Sam Dyson and Ken Mularski, whose help in getting this project off the ground was pivotal, and whose guidance throughout was essential. Thank you to Eileen Murphy for the same. I have a great deal of gratitude for the entire Payton community, from the security officers at the front desk to principal Gail Ward, for the kindness they showed me all year.

This book had many readers. My thanks to Austin Bunn, Janice P. Nimura, and Barney Latimer for the care they brought to the text. Thanks also to Kevin Delaney, Jordan Henry, Joshua Spanogle, Mark Holtzen, Clark McKown, Carey Bartell, and

Josh Gilbert, for their comments and their high school reminiscences (or was that dread?).

Thank you to my editor, Lauri Hornik, both for the initial idea, and for the patience in bringing it to fruition. Thanks to the art director Lily Malcom for her clear eyes, to Regina Castillo for her sharp copyediting, and to everyone in the Dial Books family.

Thanks, as always, to my agent, Liz Darhansoff.

Lastly, thank you to Elise Cappella, for the daily insight, for listening to all the stories I came home with. And to Zoë and Mia, you will be in high school someday, though not so soon.

Elisha Cooper went to high school in Connecticut, graduated from Yale, then worked for *The New Yorker* before becoming a writer and illustrator. He is the author of the memoir *Crawling: A Father's First Year* and many children's books, including *Beach*, *A Good Night Walk*, and *Dance!* which was a *New York Times* Ten Best Illustrated winner.

Elisha lives in New York City with his wife and two daughters.